Springer Series
on Family Violence

Albert R. Roberts, PhD, Series Editor

John S. Wodarski, PhD, is the Director of the Doctoral Program and of the Research Center, and is Janet B. Wattles Research Professor, at the School of Social Work of the State University of New York at Buffalo.

Lois A. Wodarski is a Clinical Associate Professor in the Department of Social and Preventive Medicine of The School of Medicine of the State University of New York at Buffalo.

Lisa A. Rapp, CSW, is a doctoral candidate in the School of Social Work of the State University of New York at Buffalo.

Preventing Teenage Violence

An Empirical Paradigm For Schools And Families

John S. Wodarski, PhD
Lois A. Wodarski, PhD

 Springer Publishing Company

Springer Publishing Company, Inc.
536 Broadway
New York, NY 10012-3955

Cover design by Margaret Dunin
Acquisitions Editor: Bill Tucker
Production Editor: T. Orrantia

98 99 00 01 02 / 5 4 3 2 1

Library of Congress Cataloging-in-Publication-Data

Wodarski, John S.
    Preventing teenage violence: an empirical paradigm for schools and
families / John S. Wodarski, Lois A. Wodarski.
        p.   cm.
    Includes bibliographical references and index.
    ISBN 0-8261-1188-2
    1. Teenagers—United States—Attitudes.   2. Violence in children—
United States—Prevention.   I. Wodarski, Lois Ann.   II. Title.
HQ796.W58   1998
362.7—dc21   97-38766
                                                                  CIP

Printed in the United States of America

Contents

v

96671

Foreword

In all its manifestations and consequences, violence—especially among teenagers—is a growing and serious problem in this country and world-wide. That youth violence deserves public attention is widely understood. Less understood are the causes, origins, and antecedents of violent behavior. Even more baffling is how to address this problem through responsive programs aimed at teenagers, their families, and their schools.

What form should those programs take? Who should pay for them and deliver them? Where does the locus of responsibility lie for treating and, more important, for preventing youth violence? Are local governments responsible, or are problems of violence sufficiently severe to command federal intervention? Does the media play a role in fomenting youth violence and, if so, in what ways can the media better serve its youthful consumers and the larger citizenry by decrying violence. These and myriad other questions give a hint of the challenges facing behavioral scientists who develop, implement, and evaluate programs aimed at preventing teenage violence in America.

Professors John and Lois Wodarski have risen to those challenges in preparing their approach to dealing with teenage violence through intervention in schools and families. In so doing, the authors contribute significantly to scientific knowledge on theory-based, empirically grounded intervention programs for dealing with youth violence. The program described in careful detail in this book is not only clinically responsive, but also scientifically defensible in its reliance on tested, proven methods developed by the authors and others in addressing a host of problems among youth. Drawing on a long and distinguished body of research issuing from their own group and from a small but productive core of like-minded scientists, Professors John and Lois Wodarski have put forth a useful compendium.

The book includes a description of a complete prevention program and a rigorous battery of assessment measures to help clinicians and researchers plan and evaluate the delivery of their own youth violence prevention efforts that adapt wholly or in part the Wodarskis' approach. Using the book, practitioners and investigators can palpably advance the available knowledge base on intervention approaches to deal effectively with problems of violence among young people.

Toward stimulating those efforts, this book performs a sorely needed service. Yet, much more work remains to be done. Only by applying such programs and evaluation paradigms as the Wodarskis have put forth can we begin to impact youth violence. The impressive material in this book must reach the hands of teachers, social workers, counselors, and concerned parents who desperately seek thoughtful and promising solutions to teenage violence.

John and Lois Wodarski have done their part in making publicly available the latest knowledge and techniques for combating youth violence. Now the task falls to you and me to carry that knowledge and those techniques into the field in the service of helping America's youth reach their full potential and altogether avoid becoming perpetrators and victims of violence.

Steven Schinke, PhD, Professor
Graduate School of Social Work
Columbia University
New York
September, 1997

Chapter 1

Introduction

A dolescent violence has risen dramatically in the last decade and, along with sexual activity, is now considered the most signifi-cant risk factor for dysfunctional behavior among those in this age group (Feindler & Ecton, 1986; Krueger et al., 1994; Vanderschmidt et al., 1993; Wodarski & Hendrick, 1987). Tragically, violence is tak-ing its toll of our nation's young people. During the past two decades, the homicide rate has doubled and the suicide rate has tripled among 10- to 14-year-olds. At present, 75% of deaths occurring among 10- to 19-year-olds are the result of violence and injury. Among African-Americans 15 to 19 years old, homicide is the leading cause of death (Wodarski & Wodarski, 1993). Adolescents' involvement in violent crime has become a grave concern throughout the nation. For the past several decades, the number of young people involved in crimes involving vio-lence has increased. Additionally, the number involved in violent crimes at an earlier age is increasing. From 1989 to 1994, the arrest rate for violent crimes (murder, rape, robbery, and assault) rose over 46% among teenagers, compared with 12% among adults. In terms of arrest rates per 100,000 population, 14- to 17-year-olds have now surpassed young adults ages 18 to 24 (Fox, 1996).

By the year 2005, the number of people ages 14 to 17 will increase by 20%. Even if the per capita rate of homicide among teenagers remains the same, the number of 14- to 17-year-olds who will commit murder will increase to nearly 5,000 annually because of changing demograph-ics (Fox, 1996).

Guns—and specifically handguns—have played a major role in the surge of murder among juveniles (Snyder, Sickmund, & Poe-Yamagata,

1

1996). Since 1985, arrests for gun-related homicide are up 80% among White juveniles and 120% among Black juveniles (Fox, 1996). Moreover, it is believed that these arrest statistics underestimate the number of offenses committed. Research also demonstrates that among the small group of juvenile offenders who commit these crimes, a substantial proportion continue to commit crimes as adults (Hamparian, Davis, Jacobson, & McGraw, 1985; Rapp & Wodarski, in press).

Despite the concern over violence among our young people, we have made little headway in combating the problem. Researchers have explored every theoretical focus, from social to neurological, related to antisocial behavior of youngsters. Because a large number of background factors—such as unemployment, peers, stress, low socioeconomic status, marital problems, physical problems, and neighborhood—are believed to contribute to the problem, researchers often feel that in focusing on any single aspect, they will lose validity, accuracy, and applicability to real life (Earls, 1994; Feldman, Caplinger, & Wodarski, 1983; Gibbons, 1986).

Providing services to potentially violent children has been a major focus for human service practitioners. Various theories, such as psychoanalysis and behaviorism, have attempted to explain violent behavior. Additionally, a variety of treatment modalities, such as intensive individual and group residential treatment and family therapy, have been proposed (Curry, 1985). Research indicates that violent children are one of the most troublesome groups in terms of provision of services (Kazdin, 1985, 1987). The problems of violent children are not resolved by current interventions, and interventions are costly in terms of length of incarceration and expenditures on services.

The concept of violent behavior is vague. In this chapter, we focus on acts that are of greatest concern to human service workers: violent behavior that involves an intent to do physical harm to other individuals—specifically rape, murder, and physical assault.

AGE OF ONSET AND FREQUENCY OF VIOLENT BEHAVIOR

Data indicate that the earlier an adolescent's age at his or her first arrest, the greater the probability of future violence (Elliott, 1994). For example, one study found that when the age at first arrest was between 8 and 10, the mean number of violent offenses for an individual was 0.25. Furthermore, 20% of those classified as recidivists by age 18 were involved in violent crime as adults (Howell, Krisberg, & Jones, 1995; Moffitt, in press).

Violent offenders tend to commit more crimes than other offenders. Moreover, as an adolescent commits more offenses, it becomes more likely that the offenses will be violent. Of males charged with 18 or more offenses, about 10% have committed at least one violent act. Furthermore, while all other index offenses (such as robbery) either decrease or are unaffected by age, violence shows an increase with age.

There is evidence of the development of a criminal career over time, which can lead to the commission of a violent crime. Thus, there is a substantial link between juvenile crime and adult crime. Data suggest that the violent offender is a chronic adult criminal or recidivist who began committing crimes at an early age (possibly as early as age 8), who engages in a high number of crimes, and who commits a wide variety of crimes. A small proportion of violent chronic offenders account for a large proportion of all arrests (Farrington & West, 1990; Shaffer, Water, & Adams, 1994).

CRITICAL VARIABLES IN THE DEVELOPMENT OF VIOLENT BEHAVIOR

Child Rearing

One of the most significant variables in the development of violent behavior is the lack of appropriate parenting (McCord, 1991; Rapp & Wodarski, in press; Vuchinich, Bank, & Patterson, 1992). For example, parental laxness (lack of monitoring or discipline) is significantly correlated with delinquency (Wilson, 1980). Families classified as lax were likely to have a delinquency rate more than seven times that of the families classified as strict. Likewise, Patterson and Stouthamer-Loeber (1984) found significant correlations between measures of parental monitoring and discipline and a variety of delinquent behaviors. Kazdin (1995) posited that chronically violent youngsters are found in homes where parental management skills are chronically disrupted or where the children are overmonitored or undermonitored. Parental aggression, lack of supervision, conflict, and lack of maternal affection all contribute to criminal behavior (Hawkins, Catalano, & Brewer, 1995). According to Patterson and Dishion (1985), family rejection leads to the adoption of deviant responses and is associated positively with long-term criminality.

Additional data indicate that violent children usually come from violent families (Burman & Allen-Meares, 1994). The theory is that violent children have observed parents resolve conflicts by violent means and have learned to solve their own conflicts in this way. Violence is thus modeled as a problem-solving strategy. Violent children also have a history of noncompliant behavior—that is, they do not respond to reasonable requests by parents (Kazdin, 1985). When children start school, coercive behaviors accelerate toward parents and, at school, toward prosocial peers and adults. Evidence has shown that children who engage in antisocial behavior can be grouped as "stealers" and "aggressors." Which type of antisocial behavior a child engages in is determined in large part by the type of parental supervision exercised (Hewitt & Jenkins, 1946; Kazdin, 1995; Loeber & Schmaling, 1985; Patterson, 1982). Stealers come from homes with insufficient monitoring and discipline, whereas aggressors come from homes in which parenting is characterized by more aversive interaction. Age also determines the type of antisocial activity in which a child engages. A younger child who hits playmates over the head with a toy may later get into fistfights and, having joined a gang, may be introduced to stealing. The authors cited posit that these behaviors form a continuum; if left unattended, the behavior will increase in frequency, range of contexts, variety, and severity.

Cognitive, Social, and Academic Skills

Because of their coercive behavior, violent children do not learn empathic behavior or adequate cognitive strategies for dealing with anger (White et al., 1994). Likewise, they do not learn to handle stress in a prosocial manner. Thus, violent children are not prepared adequately to deal with stress once they leave protected homes.

Dishion, Loeber, Stouthamer-Loeber, and Patterson (1984) found that deficient academic skills in the areas of verbal intelligence, reading, and completing homework, and mothers' ratings of academic competence, correlated most significantly with violence in adolescents. Rejection by adults and prosocial peers at school has been related significantly to violent behavior. Tremblay et al. (1992) and Kazdin (1995) postulated that lack of social or academic skills increases the child's chance of failure in school and with peers and family and thus exacerbates the child's alienation from prosocial relationships. In addition, there is a positive association between dropping out of high school and later criminality (Hawkins et al., 1995).

Self-Esteem and Peer Relations

The literature indicates that violent individuals have a poor self-concept and difficulty integrating with prosocial peer groups. Difficulties at school and rejection and abuse by parents tend to reduce their self-esteem. In addition, violent individuals usually are physically unattractive, and this contributes to poor self-esteem and rejection by peers (Agnew, 1984; Hanson, Henggeler, Haefele, & Rodick, 1984; Vuchinich, Bank, & Patterson, 1992).

Violent individuals usually are not in the mainstream of prosocial peer culture. They do not form attachments to prosocial institutions; instead, they are part of a small group of peers who reinforce each other's violent behavior. According to Hirschi's control theory (1969), young people who lack adequate attachments to school and parents are "free" to engage in delinquent behavior. Delinquent peers have been found to support participation in delinquent acts through positive reinforcement (Hawkins et al., 1995).

Findings in one study showed that parents' reports of adolescent males' participation in a delinquent peer group most consistently predicted serious and repeated arrests among these youths (Hanson et al., 1984). Indeed, association with delinquent peers was found to be most prevalent among those officially classified as delinquents by law enforcement agencies (Grove & Crutchfield, 1982). Analyses strongly suggest that membership in a delinquent peer group is a strong predictor of subsequent increases in violent behavior (Goldstein & Soriano, 1994; Patterson & Dishion, 1985).

Substance Abuse

Alcohol seems to be a critical influence in the development of violent behavior. Violent adolescents cannot process cognitively, nor can they manage stress. Studies have found that individuals with a propensity for aggression become more violent under the influence of psychoactive substances. Moreover, alcohol, like violence, appears to play a major role in the death of adolescents. In the United States approximately 40% of all deaths among teenagers (aged 15 to 19) occur in vehicle crashes—and of those deaths, 50% involve alcohol (U.S. Health and Human Services, 1990). It has been found that once an adolescent starts using mood-altering substances, the influence of parents decreases and the influence of peers increases (Halebsky, 1987).

Crime in Childhood

Farrington (1991) found that early aggression, theft, and lying are associated with later delinquency. Tremblay et al. (1992) found a direct causal link between disruptive behavior in first grade and delinquent behavior at age 14.

The type of violent behavior that a child displays is a product of parental management techniques—or lack of management—the age of the child, and the child's involvement in antisocial behaviors. The higher the rate at which the child participates in antisocial behaviors, the greater the child's potential for a career of violence. Thus, there is evidence to support a quantitative development of violent behavior. Certain researchers present data suggesting that potentially violent youngsters are overtly antisocial at preschool age (Moffitt, in press).

Transition to Adult Crime

Data suggest that antisocial and delinquent behavior is a sound basis for predicting future problems. Violent offenders, more than other offenders, tend to commit more crimes, and those who commit many offenses are more likely to be violent (Guttridge et al., 1983). Furthermore, there may be a tendency for these offenders to commit more serious crimes as they get older (Farrington, 1991).

The data also indicate that juvenile delinquency is often followed by adult crime. Farrington (1991) found a close relationship between juvenile and adult convictions. In addition, more chronic offenders as a group committed the greater proportion of crimes, and those chronic offenders were identified as the youngsters first convicted at the earliest ages.

PROFILE OF VIOLENT YOUNGSTERS

Having established a category of children who appear to be most *at risk* for entrance into an environment conducive to committing a violent act, the logical next step is to attempt to identify the children in that category most likely actually to *commit* violent acts. Adolescents prone to violence generally exhibit certain traits, including inability to deal with stress (Hains, 1992; Larson, 1992; Wodarski & Hendrick, 1987), low self-esteem (Lewinsohn et al., 1993; Wodarski & Hendrick, 1987), lack of integration with peers (Coie & Jacobs, 1993; Gertstein & Briggs, 1993), substance abuse (Milgram, 1993; Marohn, 1992); and exposure to family discord (Calicchia et al., 1993).

In a study by Loeber and Schmaling (1985) comparing fighters, stealers, and "versatile" youngsters (children who fight and steal), the versatile young people scored highest, meaning that they committed the greatest variety of crimes. Furthermore, they had a higher rate of association with delinquent peer groups, had a more negative outlook on life, and were more hyperactive and disobedient. They came from homes with the poorest parental management techniques and were the most disturbed on measures of family processes, specifically lack of monitoring; inconsistent application of rules; poor supervision, reasoning, and communication; and rejection by the mother.

Patterson (1982) found that similarities and differences between fighters and stealers included noncompliance, arrested socialization (maximization of immediate gains at someone else's expense, uncontrolled impulses); reduced responsiveness to social stimuli (unresponsiveness to ordinary social reinforcers and to threats and scolding, attentional deficits); and deficits in skills (academic achievement, work, peer relations; Tremblay et al., 1992).

Violent youngsters typically have low IQs and assaultive tendencies, such as instigating fights and defying authority, and exhibit cruelty and malicious mischief. They are depressed and frustrated, feel inadequate, lack inhibitions, and expect immediate gratification. They more often come from low-income neighborhoods, witness violent acts, and are subjected to parental abuse (although not necessarily physical abuse; Yoshikawa, 1994).

MODEL OF PREVENTION

Treatment: Components of a Preventive Paradigm

We believe that early identification and intervention based on empirical knowledge with youngsters exhibiting high rates of antisocial behavior would be most instrumental in preventing delinquency. Parents must be taught adequate parenting skills, with emphasis on communication. This approach should alleviate the deleterious circumstances that affect potentially violent children. These children can be identified by an inflated rate of antisocial behavior or through violations of the law. Children must be taught life skills in the following areas: cognitive control of anger, problem solving, enhancement of peer relationships, and education about substance abuse (Borduin et al., 1995; Fiendler & Ecton, 1986; Kaplan, Konecni, & Novaco, 1984; Spence & Marziller, 1981). By introducing interventions both at home and at school, it can be determined which are most effective, either singularly or in combination, in helping aggressive youngsters overcome their antisocial tendencies.

Treatment is proposed for antisocial children—children characterized by noncompliant activities in preschool and early elementary school; restlessness; impulsivity; coercive exchanges with parents, siblings, and peers; and aggression. Data indicate that if intervention does not occur during this period, the probability that the behaviors will be chronic is increased (Wolf, Braukmann, & Ramp, 1987). Groups are used as the focus of service.

Behavioral Group Work

Despite the recent emphasis on group work, relatively few clients are treated in this manner as compared with those treated individually. Services provided to children in groups have several positive aspects:

1. The group interaction typifies many kinds of daily interactions. Services facilitating behaviors that enable people to interact in groups are likely to prepare them better for participation in larger society; that is, the interaction will help them learn the social skills necessary to secure reinforcement (Feldman & Wodarski, 1975).
2. If a behavior is learned in a group context, it is likely to come under the control of a greater number of discriminative stimuli; therefore, greater generalization of the behavior can occur for a broader variety of interactional contexts.
3. Groups provide a context in which behaviors can be tested in a realistic atmosphere; that is, clients can get immediate feedback from peers on their problem-solving behaviors. Likewise, they are provided with role models to facilitate requisite social behavior.
4. Groups provide a more valid locus for accurate diagnosis and a more potent means for changing behavior (Meyer & Smith, 1977; Rose, 1977).
5. The provision of services through groups greatly increases the number of clients who can be served.
6. Groups provide peer support for prosocial behavior; children can practice and receive reinforcement for new social skills, which facilitates their acquisition. These skills in turn enhance peer relationships and increase clients' satisfaction with life.

Social workers should be trained to incorporate basic social learning principles that can be used in working with adolescents in groups (Feldman & Wodarski, 1975; Wodarski, Feldman, & Flax, 1972). Treatment objectives can be achieved through contingency contracts, positive rein-forcement (to encourage preadolescents to change their behavior), model-ing requisite behaviors, and structuring reinforcements (such as approval) that the group members can provide themselves. The comprehensive program consists of intervention with the family and at school in the fourth, fifth, and sixth grades. The intervention at school has four major compo-nents: (1) cognitive control of anger, (2) problem solving, (3) development of peer skills, and (4) education on substance abuse.

Cognitive Control of Anger

Violent individuals lack the means to control anger (Calicchia, Moncata, & Santastedaro, 1993; Davis & Boster, 1993; Gertstein & Briggs, 1993; LeCroy, 1983). Professionals must be prepared to help preadolescents develop the following skills:

1. Identify stressors that can provoke anger and subsequent vio-lent behavior.
2. Develop cognitive relaxation skills to reduce the effects of stress.
3. Learn how to receive assertive statements and deal with the anger of others.
4. Develop appropriate communication and assertion skills.
5. Practice alternative behavior, such as removal of the stimulus, in anger-provoking situations.

Problem Solving

Preadolescents who have difficulty coping with daily problems of living should be taught a problem-solving approach based on the work of D'Zurilla and Goldfried (1971), Goldfried and Goldfried (1975), Schinke and Gilchrist (1984), and Spivack and Shure (1974). The skills empha-sized are how to generate information; how to generate possible solu-tions; how to evaluate possible courses of action; and how to choose and implement strategies by understanding that certain consequences and stimuli can control problem-solving behavior, by isolating and defining a behavior to be changed, by using stimulus control techniques, by problem solving, and by using appropriate consequences to increase or decrease a behavior.

Enhancement of Peer Skills

Altering youngsters' dissatisfaction with interpersonal relationships and their perception of themselves as lacking in social skills is important in preventing violence (Mizes, Morgan, & Buder, 1990). Thus, potentially violent children must learn how to interact with others in meaningful and satisfying ways. Facets of the program developed by Lange and Jakubowski (1976) are proposed, involving training in conversational skills, use of appropriate nonverbal communication, and development of assertive behavior to decrease stress produced by inadequately met social needs.

Specific skills taught include how to introduce oneself, how to initiate and continue conversations, how to give and receive compliments, how to enhance appearance, how to make and refuse requests, how to express feelings spontaneously, and how to use appropriate nonverbal behavior to enhance sociability.

Education on Substance Abuse

Substance abuse is the last link in establishing a violent career and is a major factor in maintaining it (Milgram, 1993). Thus, children should participate in a program designed to educate them about drugs and how issues of substance abuse apply to their own lives. The program should emphasize self-management.

Basic Knowledge About Drugs.   Children must learn about drug use, including what dosage of drugs a body can absorb in a given period, and when an intoxicated person is in an emergency situation. They should also learn how to deal with such an occurrence, should understand the physiological effects of drugs and the amount of alcohol in alcoholic beverages, and should learn how to assess a drug problem.

Self-Management and Maintenance.   Children should be taught basic principles of social learning theory to enable them to manage situations involving drugs. Social learning theorists emphasize that drug abuse is learned through reinforcement. The reinforcers often include reduction of stress (lessened inhibition in sociability around peers), removal from an unpleasant situation (because adolescents tend to consume more drugs at one sitting than adults, this behavior more often results in their passing out), and an excuse for otherwise unacceptable behavior (for example, aggressive or flirtatious behavior might be excused; Wodarski, 1987).

Role-Playing Simulation Exercises.   Role-playing simulations can be used to help children practice refusing drugs in a socially acceptable manner within a normal peer context (Foy, Miller, Eisler, & O'Toole, 1976). Children can develop more effective ways of dealing with social pressures to consume drugs. Specific situations can be practiced in which some individuals apply such pressure to others. Children practice reactions to statements like these: "One drink won't hurt you." "What kind of friend are you?" "Just have a little one; I'll make sure you won't have any more."

Preventive Strategy for Families

Parents likewise must be educated about the dynamics of violent behavior. Parents must be taught problem-solving skills and communication for conflict resolution (Robin & Foster, 1984). The five steps involved in problem solving should be delineated: (1) definition of the problem, (2) generation of alternative solutions, (3) decision making, (4) planning to implement the solution, and (5) renegotiation. Parents then discuss these steps in the group and role-play use of the procedures. During the role-playing, group members attempt to solve problems of adolescents of other group members.

Information on use of positive and negative control with adolescents should be included. This material focuses on increasing positive reinforcement for appropriate behavior rather than using coercion such as negative reinforcement and punishment (Alexander, Bortin, Schiavo, & Parsons, 1976; Forehand & McMahon, 1981; Patterson, 1981).

Parents should understand that better communication skills, better problem-solving skills, and positive reinforcement will result in a better parent-child relationship and will reduce the probability of violent behavior. Additional sessions should be scheduled to support the use of these practices and to refine their implementation.

SUMMARY

The effectiveness of an interdisciplinary approach to identifying and intervening with antisocial, delinquent, and potentially violent youngsters cannot be easily measured. Given the proven ineffectiveness of previous treatments, however, this approach should be attempted.

With increased awareness of the warning signs of violent behavior, intervention in the home on a more personal, day-to-day basis might take place. Education about how to identify the warning signals and how to teach parenting skills is also necessary. Because parents and peers are primary influences on violent behavior, preventive efforts should be directed toward these two groups. Parenting models are available. The intervention proposed in this text is ambitious, but it has the potential to significantly alleviate the problems of antisocial youngsters.

We have reviewed theoretical knowledge and research about violent children. Factors that affect the development of violent behavior in children were elaborated. A prevention paradigm that uses family and school interventions in the late elementary school years was proposed as the treatment of choice.

REFERENCES

Agnew, R. (1984). Appearance and delinquency. *Criminology, 22*(3), 421–440.

Burman, S., & Allen-Meares, P. (1994). Neglected victims of murder: Children's witness to parental homicide. *Journal of the National Association of Social Workers, 39,* 28–34.

Calicchia, J. D., Moncata, S. J., & Santostefaro, S. (1993). Cognitive control differences in violent juvenile inpatients. *Journal of Clinical Psychology, 49*(5), 731–740.

Curry, J. F. (1985). Aggressive or delinquent adolescents: Family therapy interventions. *Practice Applications, 3*(1).

Dishion, T. J., Loeber, R., Stouthamer-Loeber, M., & Patterson, G. R. (1984). Skills deficits and male adolescent delinquency. *Journal of Abnormal Child Psychology, 12,* 37–54.

D'Zurilla, T. J., & Goldfried, M. R. (1971). Problem-solving and behavior modification. *Journal of Abnormal Psychology, 78,* 107–126.

Earls, F. (1991). Not fear, nor quarantine, but science: Preparation for a decade of research to advance knowledge about causes and control of violence in youths. *Journal of Adolescent Health, 12*(8), 619–629.

Elliott, D. (1994). Serious violent offenders: Onset, developmental course, and termination. *Criminology, 32,* 1–21.

Farrington, D. (1991). Childhood aggression and adult violence. In D. Pepler & K. Rubin (Eds.), *The development and treatment of childhood aggression* (pp. 5–29). Hillsdale, NJ: Lawrence Erlbaum.

Farrington, D., & West, D. (1993). Criminal, penal and life histories of chronic offenders: Risk and protective factors and early identification. *Criminal Behavior and Mental Health, 3,* 492–523.

Feindler, E. L., & Ecton, R. B. (1986). *Adolescent anger control: Cognitive-behavioral techniques.* New York: Pergamon.

Feldman, R. A., Caplinger, T. E., & Wodarski, J. S. (1983). *The St. Louis conundrum: The effective treatment of antisocial youths.* Englewood Cliffs, NJ: Prentice-Hall.

Feldman, R. A., & Wodarski, J. S. (1975). *Contemporary approaches to group treatment.* San Francisco: Jossey-Bass.

Forehand, R., & McMahon, R. J. (1981). *Helping the noncompliant child: A clinician's guide to parent training.* New York: Guilford.

Fox, A. (1996). *Trends in juvenile violence.* Washington, DC: Bureau of Justice Statistics.

Foy, C. W., Miller, P. M., Eisler, R. M., & O'Toole, O. H. (1976). Social skills training to teach alcoholics to refuse drinks effectively. *Journal of Studies on Alcohol, 37*(9), 1340–1345.

Gibbons, D. C. (1986). Juvenile delinquency: Can social science find a cure? *Crime and Delinquency, 32*(2), 186–204.

Goldfried, M., & Goldfried, A. (1975). Cognitive change methods. In F. Kanfer and A. Goldstein (Eds.), *Helping people change.* New York: Pergamon.

Goldstein, A., & Soriano, F. (1994). Juvenile gangs. In L. Eron, J. Gentry, & P. Schlegel (Eds.), *A reason to hope: A psychosocial perspective on violence and youth* (pp. 315–336). Washington, DC: APA.

Grove, W. R., & Crutchfield, R. D. (1982). The family and juvenile delinquency. *Sociological Quarterly, 23,* 301–319.

Hains, A. A., (1992). Comparison of cognitive-behavior stress management techniques with adolescent boys. *Journal of Counseling and Development, 70*(5), 600–605.

Halebsky, M. (1987). Adolescent alcohol and substance abuse: Parent and peer effects. *Adolescence, 22,* 88, 961–967.

Hamparian, D. M., Davis, J. M., Jacobson, J. M., & McGraw, R. E. (1985). *The young criminal years of the violent few.* Washington, DC: U.S. Department of Justice, Office of Juvenile Justice and Delinquency Prevention.

Hanson, C. L., Henggeler, S. W., Haefele, W. F., & Rodick, J. D. (1984). Demographic, individual, and family relationship correlates of serious and repeated crime among adolescents and their siblings. *Journal of Consulting and Clinical Psychology, 52*(4), 528–538.

Hawkins, J., Catalano, R., & Brewer, D. (1995). Preventing serious, violent, and chronic juvenile offending: Effective strategies from conception to age 6. In J. Howell, B. Krisberg, J. Hawkins, & J. Wilson (Eds.), *Serious, violent, and chronic juvenile offenders* (pp. 47–60). Thousand Oaks, CA: Sage.

Hewitt, L. E., & Jenkins, R. L. (1946). *Fundamental patterns of maladjustment: The dynamics of their origin.* Lansing, MI: Michigan Child Guidance Institute.

Hirschi, T. (1969). *Causes of delinquency.* Berkeley: University of California.

Howell, J., Krisberg, B., & Jones, M. (1995). Trends in juvenile crime and youth violence. In J. Howell, B. Krisberg, J. Hawkins, & J. Wilson (Eds.), *Serious, violent, and chronic juvenile offenders* (pp.1–35). Thousand Oaks, CA: Sage.

Kaplan, R. M., Konecni, V. J., & Novaco, R. W. (Eds.), (1984). *Aggression in children and youth (NATO Advanced Science Institute Series, Behavioral and Social Sciences, No. 17).* The Hague, Netherlands: Martinus Nijhoff.

Kazdin, A. (1995). *Conduct disorders in childhood and adolescence* (2nd ed.). Thousand Oaks, CA: Sage.

Kazdin, A. E. (1985). *Treatment of antisocial behavior in children and adoles-*

cents: Alternative interventions and their effectiveness. Homewood, IL: Dorsey Press.

Kazdin, A. E. (1987). Treatment of antisocial behavior in children: Current status and future directions. *Psychological Bulletin, 102*(2), 187–203.

Krueger, R. F., Schmutte, P. S., Caspi, A., Moffitt, T. E., Campbell, K., & Silva, P. A. (1994). Personality traits that are linked to crime among men and women: Evidence from a birth cohort. *Journal of Abnormal Psychology, 103*(2), 328–338.

Lange, A. J., & Jakubowski, P. (1976). *Responsible assertive behavior*. Champaign, IL: Research Press.

Larson, J. D. (1992). Anger and aggression management techniques through the Think First curriculum. *Journal of Offender Rehabilitation, 18*(1–2), 101–117.

LeCroy, C. W. (1983). Social-cognitive group work with children. *Behavior Group Therapy, 5*(1), 91–116.

Lefkowitz, M., Eron, L., Walsder, L., & Huesmann, L. R. (1977). *Growing up to be violent: A longitudinal study of the development of aggression*. New York: Pergamon.

Lewinsohn, P. M., Rohde, P., Seeley, J. R. (1993). Psychosocial characteristics of adolescents with a history of suicide attempts. *Journal of the American Academy of Child and Adolescent Psychiatry, 32*(1), 60–68.

Loeber, R. (1982). The stability of antisocial and delinquent child behavior: A review. *Child Development, 53,* 1431–1446.

Loeber, R., & Schmaling, K. B. (1985). The utility of differentiating between mixed and pure forms of antisocial child behavior. *Journal of Abnormal Child Psychology, 13*(2), 315–336.

McCord, J. (1991). The cycle of crime and socialization practices. *The Journal of Criminal Law and Criminology, 82,* 211–228.

Meyer, R. G., & Smith, S. S. (1977). A crisis in group therapy. *American Psychologist, 32,* 638–643.

Milgram, G. G. (1993). Adolescents, alcohol, and aggression. *Journal of Studies on Alcohol,* (supp.), 53–61.

Moffitt, T. (in press). Adolescence-limited and life-course persistent antisocial behavior: A developmental taxonomy. *Psychological Review.*

Patterson, G. R. (1981). *Coercive family process*. Eugene, OR: Castalia.

Patterson, G. R. (1982). *Coercive family process* (Vol. 3). Eugene, OR: Castalia.

Patterson, G. R., & Dishion, T. J. (1985). Contributions of families and peers to delinquency. *Criminology, 23*(1), 63–79.

Patterson, G. R., & Stouthamer-Loeber, M. (1984). The correlation of family management practices and delinquency. *Child Development, 55,* 1299–1307.

Rapp, L., & Wodarski, J. (in press). Juvenile violence: Its high risk factors, current interventions and implications for social work practice. *Journal of Applied Social Sciences.*

Robin, A. L., & Foster, S. L. (1984). Problem-solving communication training: A behavioral family systems approach to parent-adolescent conflict. In P. Karoly, & J. Steffen (Eds.), *Adolescent behavior disorders: Foundations and contemporary concerns* (pp. 195–240). Lexington, MA: D. C. Heath.

Rose, S. D. (1977). *Group therapy: A behavioral approach.* Englewood Cliffs, NJ: Prentice-Hall.

Schinke, S. P., & Gilchrist, L. D. (1984). *Life counseling with adolescents.* Baltimore: University Park Press.

Snyder, H., Sickmund, M., & Poe-Yamagata, E. (1996, February). *Juvenile offenders and victims: 1996 update on violence.* Washington, DC: Office of Juvenile Justice and Delinquency Prevention.

Spence, S. H., & Marzillier, J. S. (1981). Social skills training with adolescent male offenders: II. Short-term, long-term and generalized effects. *Behavior Research and Therapy, 19*(4), 349–368.

Spivack, G., & Shure, M. B. (1974). *Social adjustment of young children.* San Francisco: Jossey-Bass.

Thornberry, T. P., Moore, M., & Christenson, R. L. (1985). The effect of dropping out of high school on subsequent criminal behavior. *Criminology, 23*(1), 3–18.

Tremblay, R., Masse, B., Perron, D., Leblanc, M., Schwartzman, A., & Ledingham, J. (1992). Early disruptive behavior, poor school achievement, delinquent behavior, and delinquent personality: longitudinal analyses. *Journal of Consulting and Clinical Psychology, 60,* 64–72.

United States Department of Health and Human Services. (1990). *Seventh Special Report to the U.S. Congress on Alcohol and Health (DHHS Publication No. ADH 3253).* Washington, DC: U.S. Government Printing Office.

Vanderschmidt, H. F., Lang, J. M., Knight-Williams, V., & Vanderschmidt, G. F., (1993). Risks among inner-city young teens: The prevalence of sexual activity, violence, drugs, and smoking. *Journal of Adolescent Health, 14*(4), 282–288.

Vuchinich, S., Bank, L., & Patterson, G. (1992). Parenting, peers, and the stability of antisocial behavior in preadolescent boys. *Developmental Psychology, 28,* 510–520.

White, J. E., Moffitt, T. E. Caspi, A., Bartusch, D. J., Needles, D. J., & Stouthamer-Loeber, M. (1994). Measuring impulsivity and examining its relationship to delinquency. *Journal of Abnormal Psychology, 103*(2), 192–205.

Wilson, H. (1980). Parental supervision: A neglected aspect of delinquency. *British Journal of Criminology, 20*(3), 203–235.

Wodarski, J. S. (1987). Evaluating a social learning approach to teaching adolescents about alcohol and driving: A multiple variable evaluation. *Journal of Social Service Research, 10*(2/3/4), 121–144.

Wodarski, J. S., Feldman, R. A., & Flax, N. (1972). Social learning theory in group work practice with antisocial children. *Clinical Social Work Journal, 1*(2), 78–93.

Wodarski, J. S., & Hedrick, M. (1987). Violent children: A practice paradigm. *Social Work in Education, 10,* 28–42.

Wodarski, J. S., & Wodarski, L. A. (1993). *Curriculums and practical aspects of implementation: Preventive health services for adolescents.* Lanham, MD: University Press of America, Inc.

Wolf, M. M., Braukmann, C. J., & Ramp, K. A. (1987). Serious delinquent behavior as a part of a significantly handicapping condition: Cures and supporting environments. *Journal of Applied Behavior Analysis, 20,* 347–359.

Yoshikawa, H. (1994). Prevention as a cumulative protection: Effects of early family support and education on chronic delinquency and its risks. *Psychological Bulletin, 115,* 28–54.

Chapter 2

The Intervention

The multiple causes of violence in adolescence necessitate a multi-faceted approach to intervention (England & Cole, 1992; Marohn, 1992). As described in chapter 1, this program intervenes in four areas: management of anger and stress, problem solving, enhancement of peer skills, and education about substance abuse. Within education about drugs, the components are basic knowledge, self-management and maintenance, and role-playing. The present chapter elaborates on some of these.

MANAGEMENT OF ANGER AND STRESS

Adolescents' violence is most often triggered by inability to manage anger (Gerstein & Briggs, 1993; Larson, 1992). Therefore, the program's first unit deals with managing anger and stress. The unit includes relaxation training, learning the physical cues of the anger response, and using those cues to begin the relaxation response. Participants also learn how to recognize specific stimuli—triggers—for their anger (Wodarski & Wodarski, 1993; White et al., 1994).

This unit also includes training in skills of communication and assertiveness. Anger is an emotion that frequently is expressed interpersonally (Larson, 1992). Assertiveness training provides adolescents with the

skills necessary to express their anger appropriately. In addition, assertiveness can help adolescents resist negative peer influence, which has
also been shown to contribute to violent behavior (Coie & Jacobs, 1993).
Recent research has shown that aggressive children tend to minimize
the effects of their behaviors on others (Herzberger & Hall, 1993). This
program ameliorates that problem through the development of communication and active listening skills.

The link between the anger response and cognition is well established. It has been clearly shown that as well as being a biological reflex,
anger also can be induced by cognition such as personal memories and
beliefs (Davis & Boster, 1993; Mizes, Morgan, & Buder, 1990). The self-
instruction unit breaks down angry reactions into component parts (Davis
& Boster, 1993). Cognitive responses applicable to each component
are then taught to the participants. That technique allows them to gain
new coping abilities in addition to being able to apply previously learned
techniques (Wodarski & Wodarski, 1993). The unit concludes with a
section that enables participants to integrate the material more fully.

EDUCATION ABOUT SUBSTANCE ABUSE

The initial unit on anger will be followed by a unit dealing with substance abuse among adolescents. There is a strong correlation between
adolescents' use of drugs and alcohol and violent behavior (Marohn,
1992; Weishew & Perg, 1993). The second phase of this approach
serves to follow up and reinforce the unit on anger by educating participants about drugs and alcohol, as well as helping them to develop
the skills necessary to resist influences that may steer them toward
substance abuse.

Adolescence is the developmental stage in which experimenta-
tion with mood-altering substances is most active (Kagen, 1991;
Novacek, Raskin, & Hogan, 1991). Short-term consequences of adolescents' substance abuse include premature death in traffic and other
accidents, antisocial behavior and its consequences, suicide, increased
risk of HIV infection, and school-related difficulties (Oetting & Beauvais,
1990). Long-term consequences of substance abuse in adolescence
also include health problems later in life, failure to prepare adequately
for adulthood, and problems resulting from arrests while intoxicated
(Kagan, 1991; Oetting & Beauvais, 1990; Vander & Damirjian, 1990;
Wodarski & Feit, 1995).

The primary developmental tasks of adolescence are establishing autonomy and forming an identity. As a result, adolescents begin to separate from their parents and test new philosophies, value systems, and lifestyles (Kaplan & Sadock, 1991). For many adolescents, the process of achieving autonomy creates feelings of bewilderment, stress, and turmoil. Those emotions often cause adolescents to view mood-altering chemicals as one of their few satisfying choices in life (Kipke, Montgomery, & MacKenzie, 1993; Wagner, 1993). By the late 1980's, 75% of high school students were using mood-altering substances regularly, and 85% of those were using these substances at least three times per week (Martin, Arria, Mezzrich, & Bukstein, 1993; Novacek et al., 1991).

During adolescence, individuals begin to rely more heavily on peers, rather than family, for support and guidance. During this period, the need to gain approval from peers becomes paramount (Mitic, 1990; Shilts, 1991). As a result, peer influence is one of the most important factors in the initiation of chemical abuse (Coombs, Paulson, & Richardson, 1990; Mitic, 1990; Swadi, 1992). In addition, it has been found that once the adolescent starts using mood-altering substances, the influence of parents decreases further, and the influence of peers increases (Halebsky, 1987). As a child moves into adolescence, parent–child communication begins to decrease in frequency and effectiveness. Perceived and actual conflict increases during this period (Hall, 1987; Hops, Tildesley, Lichtenstein, Ary, & Sherman, 1990; Jones & Houts, 1992; Kafka & London, 1991). These factors highlight the importance of family and peers in drug prevention programs for adolescents.

Until recently, little was known about the effective prevention of substance abuse among adolescents. However, current research has begun to point toward a model for prevention that holds great promise (Norman & Turner, 1993)—a multifaceted ecological approach to dysfunctional behavior. In the past, prevention programs have tended to address only one or two facets of adolescents' problems. Reviews of these programs found that participants did not retain knowledge or skills (Dryfoos & Dryfoos, 1993; Resnicow & Botvin, 1993). Multifaceted programs have been shown to be considerably more effective. The intervention proposed here includes the following multifaceted components: alcohol and drug education utilizing peer counseling and modeling, training in social skills, relaxation techniques, and training for parents, provided in a community context (Dryfoos & Dryfoos, 1993; Logan, 1991; Lorian & Ross, 1992; Niehoff & Mensch, 1991; Silverman, 1990; Sweet, 1991).

METHOD OF DELIVERY TO ENSURE
MAINTENANCE OF SKILLS

The technique utilized in this program is based largely on social learning theory (Norman & Turner, 1993; Silverman, 1990). This theory views adolescents' behavior, both positive and negative, as being learned by modeling and reinforcement within the context in which the individual functions (parents and peers; Wodarski, 1990). Behavior is modeled by engaging in actions after having observed them in others, from whom the observer infers guidelines. It is thus distinct from simple imitation. Patterns of behavior are acquired through this process (Norman & Turner, 1993; Resnicow & Botvin, 1993). If the role models in adolescents' social context lack adequate skills in communication or cognition (or both), their behavior patterns are more likely to be maladaptive. As a result, the individual adolescent is at a much higher risk of substance abuse and violent behavior because he or she lacks the necessary behaviors to function adequately (Norman & Turner, 1993).

The method employed in both the anger management component and the substance abuse component is known as *teams-games-tournaments* (TGT). This method emphasizes group over individual achievement and uses peer influence as a teaching device. Furthermore, TGT employs games as teaching tools and utilizes small groups in a task-and-reward framework (Chambers & Abrami, 1991; Wodarski & Wodarski, 1993). By using peer influence in a positive way (Swadi & Zeitlin, 1988), TGT capitalizes on one of the primary elements in an adolescent's life, thereby increasing social attachments and facilitating the acquisition of knowledge and behavior change (Wodarski & Wodarski, 1993).

Recent research (Chambers & Abrami, 1991; Niehoff & Mensch, 1991; Wodarski, 1988) has found that small group techniques, and particularly TGT, are highly effective in preventing alcohol and drug abuse. When compared with those receiving traditional instruction or no instruction, participants receiving TGT instruction obtained superior results on the self-report indices: knowledge of drugs and alcohol, reduction in drinking, positive shifts relating to drinking and driving, reduced impulsivity, and improved self-concept. Participants viewed the program as positive and productive, and 2-year follow-up studies have found that all knowledge and attitudes gained by TGT were maintained (Wodarski, 1988; Wodarski & Bordnick, 1994).

Research has documented that the most important agent of socialization in an adolescent's life is his or her peers. The use of small peer groups in the classroom has been proved empirically to be an effective method of addressing problems and improving learning of new skills (Wodarski & Wodarski, 1993). The group context offers important benefits over teaching individually. High-risk behaviors such as substance abuse most generally occur in a group setting. Immediate peer feedback in the group setting acts as a reinforcer of new behaviors. Also, the group forum provides a realistic educational setting for students to practice interpersonal skills that can be carried over into other aspects of their lives. Social isolation, a frequent problem for youngsters at risk, is lessened through the group structure. Finally, a greater number of students may be served effectively through the group format (Wodarski & Wodarski, 1993).

The TGT technique has been developed and been found effective in the adolescents' classrooms. According to its developer—and this is supported in research data—TGT is especially helpful in teaching adolescents about high-risk behavior. It is also helpful in teaching adolescents how to make better decisions regarding these behaviors. With TGT, all students have an opportunity to succeed, because they all compete against members of other teams who are at similar levels of achievement. Points earned by low achievers are just as valuable to the overall team as points earned by high achievers.

In the beginning phase of TGT, students are given a pretest to gauge their knowledge of the material to be covered in the intervention. The results of this pretest provide the basis for dividing the classroom into four-member teams. Teams are organized according to how the students have ranked on the test. Each team has one high achiever (a student who demonstrated a high level of knowledge on the pretest), two middle achievers, and one lower achiever. This ensures, as far as possible, that the average level of achievement is approximately equal across teams.

In the games phase of TGT, students compete against members of other teams on instructional games that are provided in the TGT curriculum guide. These games are usually short-answer questions that have been designed to assess and reinforce the material covered in the classroom.

Weekly tournaments provide a forum for students to compete against other teams. Each student is assigned to a tournament table where he or she competes against two other students, each representing a different team. The students at each table are of comparable achievement levels, as determined by the pretest. Points are earned for each game question that is answered correctly, and at the end of the tournament, the top, middle, and low scores get a fixed number of points. In addition, each player receives points for participating in the tournament. The points a student earns are tabulated and used to determine if the student will move up to the next higher table with higher-achieving students, or move down to the next lower table, or stay at the same table for the next tournament. This procedure encourages students to perform at their highest level and to keep working. Each individual score is added to the scores of the other team members to compute the final score for the team.

In a typical class, students participate in two phases of the TGT curriculum designed to address substance abuse and anger. The educational units are provided in the curriculum guide for 50 minutes each day for a 13-week period. Again, the first three days of each week are to be devoted to learning about high-risk behavior through exercises, discussions, and a variety of participatory activities. The fourth day is designed as a day for the students to practice on worksheets in their teams as preparation for the tournament (assessment), which is to be held on the fifth day of each week.

FAMILY COMPONENT

A significant factor influencing adolescents' substance use is the family. Adolescents who have a viable relationship with their parents are less involved with drugs and are less influenced by drug-oriented peers (Chassin, Pillow, Curran, & Molina, 1993; Coombs et al., 1990; Pardeck, 1991). The primary means by which parents influence adolescents' substance abuse is through modeling such behavior (Chassin et al., 1993; Mitic, 1990). In addition, negative parenting behavior can be a predictor of adolescents' substance abuse (Hops et al., 1990; Jones & Houts, 1992). This program mitigates negative parental factors—such as a highly critical attitude, poor communication, and poor problem-solving skills—by providing parents with appropriate models, skills, and expectations. Not only will the amelioration of intrafamiliar dysfunctions decrease or forestall adolescents' substance abuse; it will decrease or forestall adolescents' violence as well (Earls, 1991). The problem-solving component involves four steps: identification of the problem, development of alternative solutions, decision making, and implementation of solutions (Hops et al., 1990). The communication component involves skills that can be used for problem solving as well as in other situations (Jones & Houts, 1992). Development of those skills has been shown to increase communication and decrease conflicts (Hops et al., 1990; Jones & Houts, 1992; Wodarski & Wodarski, 1993).

SUMMARY

This program considers the individual and additive effects of educational programs for adolescents and preventive programs for parents on forestalling adolescents' violence. The TGT model will be used in the components on anger and substance abuse. The program for parents will educate them about drugs, modeling behaviors, controlling anger, and communication and problem-solving skills. This program will provide advanced capabilities to help *prevent* adolescents' violence and substance abuse. It will also advance our knowledge and understanding of preventive measures that decrease the prevalence and incidence of violent behaviors and substance abuse in adolescents.

This chapter has described four elements of the program: anger and stress management, education about substance abuse, a mechanism for ensuring maintenance of skills, and a family component. The program provides adolescents with the necessary knowledge, skills, and attitudes to overcome those influences most likely to contribute to violent tendencies and substance abuse. By utilizing a peer group, knowledge and behaviors are more likely to be acquired and maintained over time.

Intervention must provide an effective and attractive means for developing new skills and behaviors. Successful interventions will provide a format for the presentation of knowledge, and a means of practicing skills and demonstrating knowledge. In this program, the teams-games-tournaments (TGT) procedure is used to implement the components involving control of anger and education on substance abuse. The family strategy is offered concurrently with TGT.

REFERENCES

Chambers, B., & Abrami, P. C. (1991). The relationship between student team learning outcomes and achievement, causal attributions, and affect. *Journal of Educational Psychology, 83*(1), 140–146.

Chassin, L., Pillow, D. R., Curran, P. J., & Molina, B. S. (1993). Relation of parental alcoholism to early adolescent substance use: A test of three mediating mechanisms. *Journal of Abnormal Psychology, 102*(4), 533–538.

Coie, J. D., & Jacobs, M. R. (1993). The role of social context in the prevention of conduct disorder. *Development and Psychopathology, 5* (1–2), 263–275.

Coombs, R. H., Paulson, M. J., & Richardson, M. A. (1990). Peer vs. parental influence in substance use among Hispanic and Anglo children and adolescents. *Journal of Youth and Adolescence, 20*(1), 73–88.

Davis, D. L., & Boster, L. H. (1993). Cognitive-behavioral-expressive interventions with aggressive and resistant youth. *Residential Treatment for Children and Youth, 10*(4), 55–68.

Dryfoos, J. G., & Dryfoos, G. (1993). Preventing substance use: Rethinking strategies. *American Journal of Public Health, 83*(6), 793–795.

Earls, F. (1991). Not fear, nor quarantine, but science: Preparation for a decade of research to advance knowledge about causes and control of violence in youths. *Journal of Adolescent Health, 12*(8), 619–629.

England, M. J., & Cole, R. F. (1992). Prevention as targeted early intervention. *Administration and Policy in Mental Health, 19*(3), 179–189.

Gertstein, L. H., & Briggs, J. R. (1993). Psychological and sociological discriminants of violent and nonviolent serious juvenile offenders. *Journal of Addictions and Offender Counseling, 14*(1), 2–13.

Halebsky, M. A. (1987). Adolescent alcohol and substance abuse: Parent and peer effects. *Adolescence, 22*(88), 961–967.

Herzberger, S. D., & Hall, J. A. (1993). Children's evaluation of retaliatory aggression against siblings and friends. *Journal of Interpersonal Violence, 8*(1), 77–93.

Hops, H., Tildesley, E., Lichtenstein, E., Ary, D., & Sherman, L. (1990). Parent-adolescent problem-solving interactions and drug use. *American Journal of Drug and Alcohol Abuse, 16*(3–4), 239–258.

Jones, D. C., & Houts, R. (1992). Parental drinking, parent-child communication, and social skills in young adults. *Journal of Studies on Alcohol, 53*(1), 48–56.

Kafka, R. R., & London, P. (1991). Communication in relationships and adolescent substance abuse: The influence of parents and friends. *Adolescence, 26*(103), 587–598.

Kagan, J. (1991). Etiologies of adolescents at risk. *Journal of Adolescent Health, 12*(8), 591–596.

Kaplan, H. I., & Sadock, B. J. (1991). *Synopsis of psychiatry* (6th ed.). Baltimore, MD: Williams and Wilkins.

Kipke, M. D., Montgomery, S., & MacKenzie, R. G. (1993). Substance use among youth seen at a community-based health clinic. *Journal of Adolescent Health, 14*(4), 289–294.

Larson, J. D. (1992). Anger and aggression management techniques through the Think First curriculum. *Journal of Offender Rehabilitation, 18*(1–2), 101–117.

Logan, B. N. (1991). Adolescent substance abuse prevention: An overview of the literature. *Family and Community Health, 13*(4), 25–36.

Lorian, R. P., & Ross, J. G. (1992). Programs for change: A realistic look at the nation's potential for preventing substance involvement among high-risk youth. *Journal of Community Psychology* (spec. iss.), 3–9.

Marohn, R. C. (1992). Management of the assaultive adolescent. *Hospital and Community Psychiatry, 43*(5), 522–524.

Martin, C. S., Arria, A. M., Mezzrich, A. C., & Bukstein, O. G. (1993). Patterns of polydrug use in adolescent alcohol abusers. *American Journal of Drug and Alcohol Abuse, 19*(4), 511–521.

Meichenbaum, D., & Cameron, R. (1983). Stress inoculation training. In D. Meichenbaum & M. E. Jarenko (Eds.), *Stress reduction and prevention,* (pp. 115–154). New York: Plenum.

Mitic, W. (1990). Parental versus peer influence on adolescents' alcohol consumption. *Psychological Reports, 67,* 1273–1274.

Mizes, J. S., Morgan, G. D., & Buder, J. (1990). The relationship of cognitions, assertion, and anger arousal. *Journal of Cognitive Psychotherapy, 4*(4), 369–376.

Niehoff, B. P., & Mesch, D. J. (1991). Effects of reward structures on academic performance and group processes in a classroom setting. *Journal of Psychology, 125*(4), 457–467.

Norman, E., & Turner, S. (1993). Adolescent substance abuse prevention program: Theories, models, and research in the encouraging 80's. *Journal of Primary Prevention, 14*(1), 3–20.

Novacek, J., Raskin, R., & Hogan, R. (1991). Why do adolescents use drugs? Age, sex, and user differences. *Journal of Youth and Adolescence, 20*(5), 475–492.

Oetting, E. R., & Beauvais, F. (1990). Adolescent drug use: Findings of national and local surveys. *Journal of Consulting and Clinical Psychology, 58*(4), 385–394.

Pardeck, J. T. (1991). A multiple regression analysis of family factors affecting the potential for alcoholism in college students. *Adolescence, 26*(102), 341–347.

Resnicow, K., & Botvin, G. (1993). School-based substance use prevention programs: Why do effects decay? *Preventive Medicine, 22*(4), 484–490.

Schinke, S. P., Gilchrist, L. D., Smith, T. E., & Wong, S. E. (1976). Group interpersonal skills training in a natural setting: An experimental study. *Behavior Research and Therapy, 17,* 149–154.

Schinke, S. P., & Rose, S. D. (1976). Interpersonal skills training in groups. *Journal of Counseling Psychology, 23,* 442–448.

Shilts, L. (1991). The relationship of early adolescent substance use to extracurricular activities, peer influence, and personal attitudes. *Adolescence, 26* (103), 613–617.

Silverman, W. H. (1990). Intervention strategies for the prevention of adolescent substance abuse. *Journal of Adolescent Chemical Dependency, 1*(2), 25–34.

Swadi, H. (1992). Relative risk factors in detecting adolescent drug abuse. *Drug and Alcohol Dependence, 29,* 253–254.

Swadi, H., & Zeitlin, H. (1988). Peer influence and adolescent substance abuse: A promising side? *British Journal of Addiction, 83*(2), 153–157.

Sweet, E. S. (1991). What do adolescents want? What do adolescents need? Treating the chronic relapser. *Journal of Adolescent Chemical Dependency, 1*(4), 1–8.

Tavris, C. (1982). *Anger: The misunderstood emotion.* New York: Simon & Schuster.

Vander, M., & Damirjian, A. (1990). Yes—I can't—Confusion and drug use during adolescence. *New York Department of Substance Abuse Services Newsletter.* Albany, NY: Author.

Weishew, N. L., & Perg, S. S. (1993). Variables predicting students' problem behaviors. *Journal of Educational Research, 87*(1), 5–17.

White, J. E., Moffitt, T. E. Caspi, A., Bartusch, D. J., Needles, D. J., & Stouthamer-Loeber, M. (1994). Measuring impulsivity and examining its relationship to delinquency. *Journal of Abnormal Psychology, 103*(2), 192–205.

Wodarski, J. S. (1981). *Role of research in clinical practice.* Baltimore, MD: University Park.

Wodarski, J. S. (1987). A social learning approach to teaching adolescents about alcohol and driving: A multiple variable evaluation. *Journal of Social Service Research, 10*(2–4), 121–144.

Wodarski, J. S. (1988). Teaching adolescents about alcohol and driving. *Journal of Alcohol and Drug Education, 33*(3), 54–67.

Wodarski, J. S. (1990). Adolescent substance abuse: Practice implications. *Adolescence, 25*(99), 667-688.

Wodarski, J. S., & Bordnick, P. S. (1994). Teaching adolescents about alcohol and driving: A 2-year follow-up study. *Research on Social Work Practice, 4*(1), 28–39.

Wodarski, J., & Feit, M. (1995). *Adolescent substance abuse: An empirical-based group prevention health paradigm.* Binghamton, NY: Haworth.

Wodarski, J. S., Feldman, R., & Pedi, S. (1974). Objective measurement of the independent variable: A neglected methodological aspect of community–based behavior research. *Journal of Abnormal Child Psychology, 2*(3), 239–244.

Wodarski, J. S., & Wodarski, L. A. (1993). *Curriculums and practical aspects of implementation: Preventive health services for adolescents.* Lanham, MO: University Press of America.

Chapter 3

Assessment

Any intervention program should include evaluation. This chapter describes resources that we have found useful in the evaluation of the intervention proposed in this text. The measures for the assessment have been selected for their established validity and reliability as well as their ease of administration. A brief description of each measure is provided to assist professionals to choose among them.

The assessment instruments should be administered during the week prior to the prevention program, the week after the prevention program, and at 1- and 2-year follow-ups. Assessments of students occur in group formats at school or in the program settings. Students complete the measures during school hours at a time that is designated by the school. Parents complete the measures during evening meetings on four occasions: prior to the 8-week program, at the conclusion of the 8-week program, and at each follow-up session. Parents receive a letter announcing the time and date of the session. Parents who do not show up for the sessions are contacted by telephone (if possible) and rescheduled. If families have moved, the questionnaires are mailed separately to parents and adolescents for completion. Should the packets not be returned in 2 weeks, a postcard is mailed as a reminder.

MEASURES OF ASSERTIVENESS AND PROBLEM SOLVING

Self-management, as shown by assertiveness and problem solving, can be pre- and posttested by using the following inventories.

Assertiveness Scale for Adolescents (ASA)

The ASA is a 33-item scale designed for children and adolescents in grades 6 through 12. It describes 33 interpersonal situations and gives the respondent three options as to what she or he would usually do in each situation. The instrument has three purposes: (1) to obtain children's and adolescents' reports about their typical behavior, which can be used by practitioners to identify areas of interpersonal problems; (2) to screen for intervention or prevention programs; and (3) to serve as a tool for researchers investigating assertiveness. The ASA indicated a fairly good internal consistency of .76, and the test-retest reliability was quite good, with a correlation over a 4-week interval of .84.

Problem-Solving Inventory (PSI)

The PSI was developed by Heppner and Peterson (1982) to assess respondents' perception of their own behaviors and attitudes with regard to solving problems. The PSI is a 34-item instrument designed to measure how individuals believe they generally react to personal problems in their daily lives.

MEASURES FOR ASSESSING ADOLESCENTS: DEPENDENT VARIABLES

Inventories of Violent Behavior

Two measures of violent behavior are proposed: the Anger Inventory (Novaco, 1976), and the Jesness Inventory (Kelly & Baer, 1969). The Anger Inventory is a 90-item, Likert-scaled measure that presents hypothetical anger-evoking scenarios. The Jesness Inventory is a 155-item true-false questionnaire that yields 10 trait scores, including social maladjustment and manifest aggression, as well as an index predictive of asocial tendencies (the *Asocial Index*). The Jesness Inventory was designed for youngsters between 8 and 18 years old. Its scores were normed on delinquent and nondelinquent boys and girls, including subjects of lower-middle and lower socioeconomic status (SES).

Measures of Knowledge About Drugs

Two measures of knowledge of drugs are available and recommended:

(1) An inventory for pretesting and posttesting was prepared from the curriculum guide in this text (it is published in Wodarski & Feit, 1995). The pretest and posttest each contain 100 items randomly chosen from a pool of 200. (2) Thirty-six items from the Engs Inventory assess knowledge about alcohol (Engs, 1977a, b; Engs, Decoster, Larson, & McPherson, 1978). This inventory has adequate reliability and validity.

Self-Inventories

The following self-inventories are designed to measure current drug use and problem behavior related to drugs; students' attitudes and intentions regarding drugs; motivation; and peer pressure to experiment with drugs.

Engs Inventory

Self-reports of drinking are measured by 23 items of the Engs Inventory (Engs, 1977a, b).

Questionnaire on Drug Use

Items center on behavior related to drugs (28 items); psychosocial aspects of drug use (6 items); adverse reactions to marijuana (7 items); psychological health (11 items); SES and economics (8 items); deviance (6 items); accidents and hospitalization (5 items); physical health (17 items); leisure time (9 items); interpersonal relations (8 items); life satisfaction (24 items); short-term or immediate effects of drugs (10 items); and long-term effects (16 items; Lettieri, 1981). The inventory items have adequate reliability and validity.

Smart Questionnaire

This includes measures of cigarette smoking, alcohol use, and marijuana use, and intentions to use tobacco, alcohol, and marijuana, as well as measures of numerous psychosocial constructs. Reliability is in the acceptable range (Graham et al., 1984).

Substance Abuse Proclivity Scale (SAP)

This measure includes items that identify alcohol offenders and substance misusers. Acceptable reliability and validity have been established for male adolescents and young adults (MacAndrew, 1986; Colligan & Offord, 1990).

Personal Experience Inventory (PEI)

This is a multiscale measure for use in identifying problems, making refer-
rals, and recommending treatment (Winters, Stinchfield, & Henly, 1993). It
has demonstrated power in the differential diagnosis of adolescents' alcohol abuse and other drug abuse. The measure has established adequate
reliability and validity for adolescent boys and girls aged 12 to 18.

OTHER MEASURES FOR ASSESSING ADOLESCENTS

Conflict Behavior Questionnaire (CBQ)

The CBQ (Prinz, Foster, Kent, & O'Leary, 1979) consists of 75 items (parent form) or 73 items (adolescent form) measuring perceived conflict at
home. Family conflict is identified by disapproval of and complaints about
behavior. On the CBQ, parents and adolescents independently complete
yes-no ratings of items about two potential sources of complaints: (1)
general dissatisfaction with the other person's behavior and (2) evaluations of the interactions between parent and child. Two scores are comput-
ed: Higher scores represent the number of negative descriptions of the
other's behavior (*individual scale—CBQ—ind.*) and of the dyadic interaction (*dyadic scale—CBQ—dyad*). Adequate reliability and validity are
available (Prinz et al., 1979; Robin & Foster, 1984; Robin & Weiss, 1980).

Issues Checklist (IC)

The IC (Prinz et al., 1979) is an instrument designed to assess the
occurrence, frequency, and intensity of discussions of particular issues
that may arise between parent and adolescent. The IC includes 44
issues that represent potential concerns. Representative issues are fighting with brothers and sisters, use of the telephone, use of drugs, and how
to spend free time. The checklist is completed independently by each
parent and the adolescent. For each issue, the respondent is asked to
identify: (1) whether it has been discussed during the last 4 weeks (yes or
no); (2) if yes, how many times in the last month it has been discussed;
and (3) when it was discussed, how angry or intense the discussions
were (rated on a 5-point scale from 1 = calm to 5 = angry).
       By averaging across issues, one can obtain a summary score or
quantity of issues discussed, mean frequency of discussion per issue,

mean level of intensity (anger), and a weighted average of frequency and intensity. Data on the reliability and validity of this measure are provided by Prinz et al. (1979) and Robin and Weiss (1980).

Conflict Perception Ratings

This measure assesses the individual's perceptions of conflict (poor communication) in objective dyadic interactions. Six scenes based on work by Smith and Forehand (1986) are used. Themes for the scenes were chosen from the Issues Checklist (Prinz et al., 1979). Two scenes represent a low level of conflict between adolescents and parents, two scenes represent a moderate level, and two scenes represent a high level. For each level of conflict, one scene consists of a mother-adolescent interaction and one consists of a father-adolescent interaction. Originally, 20 scenes were read by pairs of actors and were recorded on audiotape. These tapes were then rated by trained observers. Each observer rated each tape on a 7-point Likert scale, assessing the amount of conflict in the interaction. On the basis of these ratings, scenes of low (rating of 1), medium (4), and high (7) conflict were selected. Individuals listen to these six scenes (which are presented in random order) and score each interaction on the 7-point Likert scale.

MEASURES FOR ASSESSING PARENTS

Parents' knowledge about alcohol, drugs, and violent behavior is assessed using a modified version of the measures for adolescents. There are also self-inventories designed to measure current drug use, any current problematic behavior related to drugs, attitudes and intentions regarding violent behavior, and motivation (see the measures above for adolescents).

Also, the following can be used (see the measures above for adolescents): *Conflict Behavior Questionnaire, Issues Checklist, Conflict (Communication) Perception Ratings.* Two specific measures for parents are described below.

Family Assessment Device (FAD)

This instrument is designed to evaluate family functioning according to the McMaster Model. This model describes structural, occupational, and transactional properties of families and identifies six dimensions of family functioning: (1) problem solving, (2) communication, (3) roles, (4) affective responsiveness, (5) affective involvement, and (6) behavior control. It measures these six dimensions and general functioning. The FAD is a 60-item questionnaire that has demonstrated fairly good internal consistency, ranging from .72 to .92. It has also demonstrated some degree of concurrent and predictive validity (Epstein, Baldwin, & Bishop, 1983).

Revised Behavior Problem Checklist (RBPC)

This instrument (Quay & Peterson, 1983) will be used to assess parents' perceptions of adolescents' deviance. After extensive analyses, four major factors have emerged from the RBPC: (1) conduct disorder, (2) socialized aggression, (3) attention problem–immaturity, and (4) anxiety-withdrawal. The factors of the 77-item scale were derived from factor analytic studies, and intercorrelation among factors has been minimized by retaining those items that loaded on only one factor. Data have been gathered on psychiatric populations (inpatient and outpatient), and normal controls that establish adequate reliability and validity for the RBPC and its factors.

REFERENCES

Bandura, A. (1969). *Principles of behavior modification.* New York: Holt, Rinehart, & Winston.

Botvin, G. J., Baker, E., Botvin, E. M., Filazzola, A. D., & Millman, R. B. (1984). Prevention of alcohol misuse through the development of personal and social competence: A pilot study. *Journal of Studies on Alcohol, 45*(16), 550–552.

Colligan, R. C., & Offord, K. P. (1990). MacAndrew versus MacAndrew: The relative efficacy of the MAC and the SAP scales for the MMPI in screening male adolescents for substance abuse. *Journal of Personality Assessment, 54,* 534–541.

Engs, R.C. (1977a). Drinking patterns and drinking problems of college students. *Journal of Studies on Alcohol, 38*(11), 2144–2156.

Engs, R.C. (1977b). Let's look before we leap: The cognitive and behavioral evaluation of a university alcohol education program. *Journal of Alcohol and Drug Education, 22*(2), 39–48.

Engs, R. C., Decoster, D., Larson, R. V., & McPherson, P. (1978). The drinking behavior of college students and cognitive effects of a voluntary alcohol education program. *National Association of Student Personnel Administration, 15*(3), 59–64.

Epstein, N. B., Baldwin, L. M., & Bishop, D. S. (1983). The McMaster family assessment device. *Journal of Marital and Family Therapy, 9,* 171–180.

Feindler, E. L., & Ecton, R. B. (1986). *Adolescent anger control: Cognitive behavioral techniques.* New York: Pergamon.

Feldman, R. A., & Wodarski, J.S. (1975). *Contemporary approaches to group treatment.* San Francisco: Jossey-Bass.

Graham, J. W., Flay, B. R., Johnson, C. A., Hansen, W. B., Grossman, L., & Sobel, J. L. (1984). Reliability of self-report measures of drug use in prevention research: Evaluation of the project smart questionnaire vs. test-retest reliability matrix. *Journal of Drug Education, 14*(2),175–193.

Hains, A. A. (1992). Comparison of cognitive-behavior stress management techniques with adolescent boys. *Journal of Counseling and Development, 70*(5), 600–605.

Hall, J. A. (1987). Parent-adolescent conflict: An empirical review. *Adolescence, 22*(88), 767–789.

Heppner, P. P., & Petersen, C. H. (1982). The development and implications of a personal problem-solving inventory. *Journal of Counseling Psychology, 29,* 66–75.

Kelly, F. J., & Baer, D. J. (1969). Jesness inventory and self-concept measures for delinquents before and after participating in outward bound. *Psychological Reports, 25*(3), 719–724.

Lange, A. J., & Jakubowski, P. (1976). *Responsible assertive behavior.* Champaign, IL: Research Press.

Lee, D., Hallberg, E. T., Slemon, A. G., & Haase, R. F. (1985). An assertiveness scale for adolescents. *Journal of Clinical Psychology, 41,* 51–57.

Lettieri, D. J. (1981). Recommendations from a science administration perspective. In USDHHS, National Institute on Drug Abuse, *Assessing marijuana consequences: Selected items,* 111–128.

MacAndrew, C. (1986). Toward the psychometric detection of substance misuse in young men: The SAP scale. *Journal of Studies on Alcohol, 47,* 161–166.

Novaco, R. W. (1985). *Anger control.* Lexington, MA: Lexington Books.

Novaco, R. W. (1976). The treatment of chronic anger through cognitive and relaxation therapies. *Journal of Consulting and Clinical Psychology, 44*(4), 681.

Prinz, R. J., Foster, S., Kent, R. N., & O'Leary, K. D. (1979). Multivariate assessment of conflict in distressed and non-distressed mother-adolescent dyads. *Journal of Applied Behavior Analysis, 12,* 691–700.

Quay, H. C., & Peterson, D. R. (1983). *Interim manual for the revised behavior problem checklist.* Unpublished manuscript.

Robin, A. L., & Foster, S. L. (1984). Problem-solving communication training with parent-adolescent conflict. *Behavior Therapy, 12,* 593–609.

Robin, A. L., & Weiss, J. G. (1980). Criterion-related validity of behavioral and self-report measures of problem-solving communication skills in distressed and non-distressed parent-adolescent dyads. *Behavioral Assessments, 2,* 339–352.

Smith, K. A., & Forehand, R. L. (1986). Parent-adolescent conflict: Comparison and prediction of the perceptions of mothers, fathers, and daughters. *Journal of Early Adolescence, 6*(4), 353–367.

Wagner, E. F. (1993). Delay of gratification, coping with stress, and substance use in adolescence. *Experimental and Clinical Psychopharmacology, 1*(4), 27–43.

Winters, K. C., Stinchfield, R. D., & Henly, G. A. (1993). Further validation of new scales measuring adolescent and other drug use. *Journal of Studies on Alcoholism, 54,* 534–541.

Chapter 4

Teaching Teenagers to Control Anger: The Teams-Games-Tournaments Method

INTRODUCTION

Overview of the Program

Anger is an emotion that can have very destructive consequences or can provide the energy to carry out positive actions. Tavris (1982) quotes the Roman philosopher Seneca, who recognized the uniquely human aspects of anger almost 2,000 years ago: "Wild beasts and all animals, except man, are not subject to anger, for while it is the foe of reason, it is nevertheless born only where reason dwells" (p. 23).

There is a compelling need for programs to help teenagers control anger—as is evidenced by the increase in the number of violent acts committed by adolescents (Feindler & Ecton, 1986; Wodarski & Hendrick, 1987). Stress, poor self-concept, inability to interact with peers, and problems with cognitive processing have been identified by Wodarski and Hendrick and Rapp and Wodarski (in press) as characteristic of violent adolescents. These elements, therefore, need to be addressed if we are to help adolescents control their anger and, subsequently, their violent behavior. The program proposed here is designed to meet this need.

The three-phase program that follows is consistent with programs espoused by others (e.g., Feindler & Ecton, 1986; Larson, 1992; Meichenbaum & Cameroon, 1983; Novaco, 1985). Also, since teenagers spend a great deal of their time in school settings—indeed, their aggressive behavior is often first noted within the context of a school—it seems appropriate that a program for controlling anger could be designed to be utilized within an educational format.

As anger is often fueled by stress, the first unit (first week) of the curriculum deals with stress. The second unit (second week) gives students a new skill they can use in dealing both with stress and with anger: By learning the physical cues of the anger response, students become able to use these cues to begin a relaxation response (Meichenbaum & Cameron, 1983). Awareness of the various triggers of anger, both indirect and direct, helps students to recognize specific stimuli.

The skills training, much of which has been adapted from Wodarski (1986), begins with a unit (third week) on communication and assertiveness. Anger is most often played out within an interpersonal context; it is a method of communicating an emotion to another person (Tavris, 1982). Assertiveness will help students to express emotional needs in a more appropriate manner. It has been found that aggressive children are likely to believe that their victims do not really suffer (Boldizar, Perry, & Perry, 1989). The component of this unit on communication skills and active listening was designed to address this concern.

The role of cognition in the anger response is important. Human anger is not only a biological reflex, but a response to internal stimuli such as memories and beliefs (Tavris, 1982). The unit on self-instruction training (week 4) breaks the angry confrontation down into specific stages (Feindler & Ecton, 1986). Students are then taught specific cognitive responses appropriate for coping with each stage.

The unit on problem solving allows students not only to learn another important skill, but to begin to pull together and apply the things they have learned.

The final unit (week 6) was designed to allow students to integrate the material more fully.

Outline of the Program: Controlling Anger and Violence

Elements

I.   *Biological, cognitive, and sociocultural determinants of anger.*
     It is important for participants to understand what anger is, where it comes from, and what we are doing when it is expressed.

II. *Self-instruction training.*
Students will learn assertiveness skills, how to communicate, cognitive techniques in anger management, coping skills, problem-solving skills, and relapse identification methods.

Curriculum Topics

I. Week 1: Define and explore the problem

   A. What is anger?
   B. The relationship between anger and stress.
   C. Identifying sources of stress.

II. Week 2: Triggers and cues of anger

   A. What are cues and triggers?
   B. Learning how we can begin to control our anger.
   C. "Attitude adjustment" hour.
   D. The ABCs of anger.

III. Week 3: Communication skills

   A. How people communicate without talking.
   B. Individual rights and empathic listening.
   C. Assertiveness training; assertiveness techniques.

IV. Week 4: Self-instruction training

   A. Self-statements and stages of confrontation.
   B. Self-statements and belief systems.
   C. The importance of self-reinforcement.

V. Week 5: Problem solving

   A. Defining positive and negative methods of coping.
   B. Methods of dealing with anger-provoking situations.
   C. Problem solving.

VI. Week 6: Wrap-up

   A. Predicting a relapse.
   B. Wrap-up and preparation for presentation.
   C. Videotape presentations.
   D. Administer or administration of pretest and posttest.

WEEK 1: DEFINE AND EXPLORE THE PROBLEM

Day 1: What Is Anger?

Focus: Define anger and its uses.

Method: Mini-lecture and discussion.

Time: One class period.

Capsule Description: This exercise is designed to help students define anger and to see that anger can be expressed in different ways by different people. They learn also that anger can be useful.

1. A mini-lecture is presented explaining that while anger is felt by all people, it will be expressed differently, depending on cultural factors and cultural learning. Help the class to learn the difference between anger and aggression. Define both concepts for the class. Anger is a hostile *feeling;* aggression is hostile *behavior* toward another person.

2. To help the class understand that anger is not a "bad" emotion, give them a list of ways that anger is useful and have each group brainstorm. Useful functions of anger include these: (a) Anger energizes us. (b) Anger allows us to express strong emotions. (c) Anger helps us to feel less vulnerable and more in control of a situation. (d) Anger can stop someone from doing something that bothers us. (e) Anger allows us to learn what kind of situations bother us so that we can avoid them. (f) Anger helps us to make necessary changes in our lives.

Day 2: The Relationship Between Anger and Stress

Focus: Explore the relationship between anger and stress.

Method: Mini-lecture; develop a chart of stress indicators.

Time: One class period.

Capsule Description: This exercise is designed to let students explore the overlapping relationship between anger and stress. Students will develop a list of *stress indicators* and discuss how there are various ways that different people can show they are stressed. The overlap between anger and stress indicators can be explored by seeing how many stress indicators would also indicate anger.

1. The mini-lecture will cover these main points:

   a. Stress can be defined as a response that occurs when, in any situation, people deal with something with which they are unfamiliar. From this definition it seems that stress is universal and that life will be full of stress because it is full of change. Possible sources of stress for students include problems at home, changing schools, dating, and academic pressures.
   b. Certain changes are positive but are still stressful because they call for us to learn how to adapt differently.
   c. Changes tend to come in clusters. One change tends to lead to other changes. This means that stress often has a tendency to "pile up." When too many changes occur too fast, and stress does pile up over a short time, we are more likely to get ill, to show outward signs of stress, or both.
   d. Stress is not all bad. We all need it—it adds zest to our lives and energizes us to reach goals. Think how boring life would be without change. Too much stress is disturbing, but healthful levels of stress will be different for each person.
   e. Stress is caused by inner and outer circumstances. Not only experiences outside of us cause stress; our inner percep-tions, or how we view a situation, will make us feel stress. For example, if you hear people in the school hallway yelling and you think that they are yelling at you, you will feel stress even if they are yelling at someone else.

2. Have the class brainstorm a list of stress indicators from A to Z. Ask them to come up with phrases or words describing how different people may react to stressful situations. Table 4.1 "Stress from A to Z" provides examples of stress indicators.

3. Once the table is completed, lead a discussion covering how diverse these indicators can be, and how many of the ways in which people show anger are also ways in which they show they are under stress. End by suggesting that one way of dealing with anger is to deal first with interpersonal stress.

Day 3: Identifying Sources of Stress

Focus: Identify sources of stress as well as indicators of both anger and stress.

Method: Small group exercise.

TABLE 4.1   Stress From A to Z

A—anxiety, arguing, apprehension, changes in appetite
B—boredom, the "blues," the "blahs," bad temper
C—crying, confusion, conflict, colds, lacking of concentration
D—depression, drugs, defensiveness, digestive upsets, discouragement
E—edginess, extra tension, extra nervousness
F—fear, forgetfulness, fatigue, frustration
G—guilt, grudges
H—hopelessness, headaches, hiding
I—insomnia, irritability, isolation
J—jitters, joylessness
K—knots in your stomach
L—loneliness, lack of concentration
M—mood swings, muscle aches
N—nagging, nervousness, nightmares
O—orneriness, being out of control
P—panic, poor judgment, pushing too hard, needing to prove yourself
    constantly
Q—quietness, questioning
R—rudeness, resentment, skin rash, restlessness
S—sulking, spacing out
T—temper, tantrums, tension
U—unhappiness, uncertainty, unproductiveness, unforgivingness
V—vague thoughts of tension, being very mad
W—weight loss or gain, worry
X—"x-tra" pounds
Y—yawning, yelling
Z—zero energy, zero tolerance

Source: Adapted from Tubesing & Tubesing, 1984.

Time: One class period.

Capsule Description: The class will break up into small groups and complete a handout consisting of short stories. The students are to identify possible sources of stress and indicators of stress. These sources and indicators, which also seem to cause anger, should be listed on the following handout.

HANDOUT

Story 1

John was late for school, so he skipped breakfast. He felt irritable because he had to rush so much this morning. On his way to his first class, in which he had a test he was really worried about, another kid bumped into him and John's books and papers were scattered everywhere. John got mad and started yelling at the other kid.

Possible sources of stress: _____

Stress indicators: _____

Stress indicators that may also signal anger: _____

Story 2

Sue's parents have been fighting with each other for a month now. Sue spends a lot of time in her room watching TV, trying to block out the noise of her parents' arguments. She is feeling pretty depressed over this. She is still doing OK in school, but her friends have noticed that she is gaining weight and that she gets a lot of headaches. They are worried about her.

Possible sources of stress: _____

Stress indicators: _____

Stress indicators that may also signal anger: _____

Story 3

Beth and her family just moved into town. Beth is still sulking because she left all her friends behind. She was just starting to get to know some cute boys, and now her parents decide to move. She doesn't care if her father's company transferred him; she's mad about leaving everything she knows behind her. Beth has even thrown some tantrums so her parents will understand how hard this is for her. The thought of starting over in a new school gives her knots in her stomach.

Possible sources of stress: _____

Stress indicators: _____

Stress indicators that may also signal anger: _____

Story 4

Larry's father has been nagging him about everything lately. Larry is not sure what's going on, but he knows that his dad is working a lot more than usual. When his dad finally does come home, he looks worried and has no energy. When his dad is not working, he seems really restless and cranky.

Possible sources of stress: _____

Stress indicators: _____

Stress indicators that may also signal anger: _____

TEAM WORKSHEET 1

1. True or false: Our lives would be much better if we had no stress at all.
2. True or false: Anger is an emotion that all people express in similar ways.
3. True or false: Aggression is a behavior that people learn to use.
4. Who will most likely feel more stress upon entering a new school?

   a. A girl who has always done really well in school, whose parents are angry because they have to drive her to the new school, and who always argue with her on the way to school.
   b. A girl who has always done moderately well in school and who really wants to prove herself in this new school both socially and academically.

5. The way you _____ others can change the amount of stress you feel in a certain situation.

   a. think about b. behave toward c. talk with d. all of the above

6. True or false: Stress and anger are caused by situations in our lives as well as by our feelings and thoughts.
7. True or false: There is a strong connection between the amount of stress a person is under and how much anger he or she is likely to experience.
8. True or false: The amount of stress a person feels will increase with the amount of change in his or her life.
9. True or false: The more we feel in control of a situation the less likely we are to feel angry or stressed out over it.
10. True or false: Angry and aggressive kids are just in a phase, and they will grow out it.
11. True or false: Anger can be defined as an emotional reaction to stress that is brought about by provoking events.
12. True or false: All people in all cultures express anger in the same way, so it is easy to tell when any person is upset.
13. True or false: Whenever people get really angry, they will act aggressively.
14. True or false: Anger is a bad emotion, and we should try not to feel it.
15. True or false: Sometimes you feel pressure or stress when someone close to you is the one who is upset.

16. Who is likely to feel more stress?

    a. A student who is facing a very difficult exam for which she has studied very thoroughly.
    b. A student who is given a moderately difficult pop quiz over material that he hasn't learned.

17. True or false: Today—as compared with the past—more teenagers are getting arrested for violent and aggressive behavior.
18. One function of anger is to _____ .
19. True or false: Everyone will see the same event as provoking or stressful.
20. Which situation will be likely to produce stress?

    a. Something good, such as your family moving to a nicer home where you can finally have your own room;
    b. Something bad, such as your favorite teacher leaving in midsemester and being replaced by a new, very stern teacher.
    c. Both a and b.

ANSWERS: TEAM WORKSHEET 1

1. False—A certain amount of stress makes us energized and productive.
2. False—People express anger in different ways, such as trying to talk with someone about it, listening to loud music, or yelling loudly.
3. True.
4. a—Stress can pile up, and there is a strong relationship between the stress we feel and major life changes added to daily problems. The girl in situation a feels pressure because she has to live up to her previous academic record as well as deal with frustrated and angry parents.
5. d
6. True—Anger and stress have inner and outer sources. Our reactions to our world can create as much stress or anger as our experiences.
7. True.
8. True—Change can be the "spice of life" up to a point, but too much change will cause us stress instead of making life interesting.
9. True.
10. False—Kids who are more aggressive than their peers will continue to be more aggressive than others as they grow up.
11. True.
12. False—In our country, people may show their anger by shouting and frowning, but this is not always true in other countries. For instance, in Japan anger is likely to be shown by excessive politeness and neutral facial expressions.
13. False—Anger and aggression are two separate behaviors. An angry mother who furiously cleans her house is angry but not aggressive. A paid assassin who calmly kills someone is acting very aggressively but is not angry.
14. False—Anger can be good when handled well. It can push us to look into unjust situations or to make needed changes in our lives.
15. True—Kids are especially likely to feel a response when their parents are upset.
16. b—It is not the difficulty of the task that makes it stressful as much as how familiar with the task the student is.
17. True—Since 1985, gun-related homicide arrests are up 80% among White juveniles and 120% among Black juveniles.
18. Energize us; express negative feelings; make us feel less

vulnerable, less helpless, and more in control of a situation; stop someone or something that bothers us; help us learn what situations provoke us so we can plan how to avoid the stress that comes with being provoked.

19. False—Not only do different people find different things stressful or provoking, but different people have different levels of stress that they can deal with.

20. c—Although different people find different things stressful, change in any form, both positive and negative, is stressful.

WEEK 2: TRIGGERS AND CUES OF ANGER

Day 1: What Are Cues and Triggers?

Focus: Define and identify cues and triggers.

Method: Mini-discussion; brainstorming a master list; and role-playing.

Time: One class period.

Capsule Description: This exercise is designed to help students identify cues and triggers for their behavior. Students will brainstorm a master list of cues and triggers (see Box 4.1, "Examples of Triggers and Cues"). Students will then break up into small groups for role-playing.

1. A mini-lecture will be presented, covering the following points:

   a. Although anger is an emotion, there are physical signs of anger that actually occur before the emotional response. These are called *cues* because they cue us to the fact that we are getting angry.

   b. We can use these physical reactions as cues to start some coping techniques, such as deep breathing. In this way we begin to learn to control our anger.

   c. *Triggers* can be thought of as events that make us angry. These can be direct or indirect. *Direct triggers* are usually things that people do to you, either in how they act or in what they say. *Indirect triggers* are things we do to ourselves—in how we view a situation—that will make us angry. Indirect triggers are often faulty perceptions of events.

2. Have the class brainstorm a master list of cues, direct triggers, and indirect triggers. Tell the class that there is a great deal of individual variation in how people experience anger. You can begin brainstorming by asking the class to think of physical signs in themselves and in other people that are cues that they are getting angry.

3. Have the class break up into small groups and give each group a situation from the master list to enact in front of the class. The class will then identify this role-playing as an example of an indirect or a direct trigger and will also identify the physical cues of anger shown in Box 4.1.

BOX 4.1

EXAMPLES OF TRIGGERS AND CUES

Physical cues of anger: Flushed face, sweaty palms, racing heart, glaring, clenching fists, grinding teeth, twitching, muscles tense.

Direct triggers: Little brother or sister goes into your room and takes something without asking, another student blames you for something that they did, someone shoving you when you are playing basketball, someone calls you names in front of your friends.

Indirect triggers: Mistakenly thinking a teacher is harder on you than on anyone else, mistakenly thinking that a group of students who are huddled together and giggling are laughing at you, making a "mountain out of a molehill," focusing on any bad things a friend has done and not remembering the good things.

Day 2: Learning How We Can Begin to Control Our Anger

Focus: Introduce the concept of self-control through selective perception.

Method: Demonstration; mini-lecture; exercise.

Time: One class period.

Capsule Description: A demonstration—"The Fool in the Ring"— is used to introduce the concept of being in control of our own behavior (see Box 4.2). A brief lecture is presented and an exercise is done in small groups to allow students to see how beliefs and interpretations of experiences can change how these experiences are perceived.

1. The demonstration begins the period.
2. A mini-lecture presents the following points:
   a. When people get extremely angry, they are actually decreasing their control over the situation.
   b. *Self-control* can be thought of as the ability people have to control their own behavior in order to reach their goals. The more of our goals we reach, the greater our sense of personal power and the better we learn to control situations instead of feeling as though situations control us.

BOX 4.2

EXERCISE: "THE FOOL IN THE RING" EXERCISE

The teacher begins by drawing a circle (or square) on the blackboard and placing an X (or object) in the middle of the circle (or square) and one on the outside (from Feindler & Ecton, 1986, pp. 89–90).

The teacher will tell the class that the X (or object) in the circle (or square) is meant to be the fool in the ring. The other person involved is the student. The fool has no power at all. This fool is in the circle only to pull the student's strings, to make the student angry. When the fool is able to do this job successfully, then the fool becomes a puppet master and the student becomes a puppet.

Fool becomes the puppet master. Student becomes the puppet.

As a result, the fool pulls the student in, and there are now two fools in the ring.

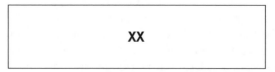

By allowing the fool to pull him or her into the ring, the student gives up power and control over the situation. The student is playing the fool's game rather than his or her own game. The students can avoid this and remain in control of the situation by cutting the string so that the fool cannot control them and cannot pull them into the circle.

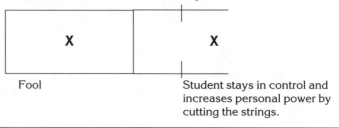

Fool   Student stays in control and increases personal power by cutting the strings.

    c. One of the ways that we use to exercise self-control—to cut the strings that the "fool" uses to control us—is to look at our interpretations of an event.

3. Exercise: "Attitude adjustment hour" (Box 4.3).

BOX 4.3

"ATTITUDE ADJUSTMENT HOUR"

Part 1

In this exercise the teacher emphasizes the role of perception in emotional responses. A handout—"Accident Report," on the following page—is passed around. Tell the class that at any moment we always have a number of different options open to us in terms of how we view a situation. The choice of that viewpoint can influence how we feel. After the class has looked at the handout, ask what is wrong with the statements and why these people may have said these things this way.

Part 2

Have the class break up into small groups. To help the class understand that it is possible to see the same situation from different viewpoints, ask each group to retell the "Attitude Adjustment" story from a different perspective. These perspectives might include:

- Soap opera, where there is a lot of drama and emotion.
- Sitcom like *Roseanne,* where everything is a joke.
- Fairy tale, where the picture of the world is rosy and magical, and everything always comes out OK.
- Sports broadcast, where things are short, to the point, and focused on action.

Part 3

After the groups have developed their stories and each group has had a chance to retell the story to the whole class, ask the class how each perspective might change and how they might react in the same situation.

HANDOUTS FOR "ATTITUDE ADJUSTMENT"

This material is adapted from Tubesing & Tubesing (1984).

Part 1: Accident Reports

Each of these is an actual statement taken from official accident reports submitted to police and insurance investigators.

- "Coming home, I drove into the wrong house and collided with a tree that shouldn't have been there."
- "The other car collided with mine without even giving warning of its intentions."
- "I collided with a stationary truck coming the other way."
- "A truck backed through my windshield into my wife's face."
- "A pedestrian hit me and went under my car."
- "The guy was all over the road. I had to swerve a number of times before I hit him."
- "I pulled away from the side of the road, glanced at my mother-in-law, and headed for the embankment."
- "As I approached the intersection, the sign suddenly appeared in a place where no sign had ever appeared before. I was unable to stop in time to avoid the accident."
- "To avoid hitting the car in front of me, I struck the telephone pole."
- "In an attempt to hit a fly, I drove into a telephone pole."
- "My car was legally parked and it backed into the other vehicle."
- "I told the police that I was not injured, but upon removing my hat, I found that I had a fractured skull."
- "The pedestrian had no idea which direction to run, so I ran over him."
- "The indirect cause of the accident was a little guy in a small car with a big mouth."
- "An invisible car came out of nowhere, struck my vehicle, and vanished."
- "I had been driving for 40 years when I fell asleep at the wheel."
- "I saw a sad-faced old gentleman as he glanced off the hood of my car."
- "I was thrown from the car as it left the road. I was later found in a ditch by some stray cows."
- "The telephone pole was approaching; I was attempting to swerve out of the way when it struck my front end."
- "I was on my way to the doctor with rear end trouble when my universal joint gave way, causing me to have an accident."

Part 2: "Attitude Adjustment" Story

When I got up this morning, I woke up 20 minutes late, so I had to rush around and get everything done really fast. My mom was downstairs trying to get my little sister to eat and they were yelling at each other so I just skipped eating and came right to school. On the way to first period I saw my boyfriend (girlfriend) flirting with someone else, and it really ticked me off. My math teacher gave a pop quiz, which I don't think I did very well on. During lunch I got a chance to see my friends and tell them about all that had happened to me. The rest of the day was pretty much OK.

Day 3: The ABCs of Anger

Focus: Introduce the concept of analysis of events using cues, triggers, and consequences.

Method: Mini-lecture; exercise.

Time: One class period.

Capsule Description: The exercise is designed to give students a chance to practice the ABCs of analyzing anger and to begin to think in terms of consequences.

    1. A mini-lecture will be given on the ABC method of situational analysis. The following points will be covered.

        a. ABC stands for antecedents, behavior, and consequences.
        b. Antecedents are things that happen before we get angry. These are like triggers.
        c. Behavior—our actual reaction when we get angry—includes cues.
        d. Consequences happen as a result of your getting angry and out of control. These may include getting into trouble, having your peers begin to avoid you, or getting hurt.

    2. Ask the class to break up into small groups.
    3. Introduce the Worksheet "Anger Police" (Table 4.2). Each group will enact a brief scene where someone gets angry. The rest of the group play the role of police who are investigating the scene. They are interested only in the facts—the actual ABCs of the situation. Ask each group to enact situations such as these:

TABLE 4.2   "Anger Police" Worksheet

| | Antecedents | | Behavior | | |
Role-Playing #	Direct Triggers	Possible Indirect Triggers	Cues	Action Taken	Consequences

a. A group of kids are picking sides for basketball teams and someone is deliberately left out.
b. A student is in the hall while there is some commotion going on. The vice-principal intervenes and that student gets into trouble for something he or she did not do.
c. A parent backs out of something that was promised a week ago, such as taking the student to a movie or shopping.
d. A group of students follow you home and make teasing remarks about you as they walk behind you.

TEAM WORKSHEET 2

1. True or false: Something someone says to you can make you angry even when the other person didn't mean what he or she said.
2. Anger releases in our bodies a hormone called _____.
3. True or false: Learning how your body signals you that you are getting angry can help you control your anger.
4. When we get angry, the feeling we have is similar to the feeling we get when we are _____.

   a. afraid b. joyful c. excited d. all of the above

5. The signal your body sends to you that you are becoming angry is called a _____.
6. People's ability to control their behavior so that they can reach their goals is called _____.
7. Anger can be caused by _____.

   a. foods we eat.
   b. someone doing something to upset you.
   c. A and B.

8. Which student will probably act angrier?

   a. One who thinks a long time about why he or she is angry and what to do about it.
   b. One who acts without thinking about it.

9. True or false: Scientists believe that anger is an emotion that has never served any purpose in our ability to survive as a species.
10. An event that provokes anger is called a _____.
11. An example of an indirect trigger is: _____

    a. Someone cutting in front of you when you're in line at McDonald's.
    b. Thinking that the teacher put you on detention because he or she hates you, when in fact it was because you broke a rule.

12. List two physical signs of anger.
13. True or false: Getting very angry and aggressive with someone else will actually give you more control over the situation.
14. What are the three steps in the ABC model of looking at anger?

15. According to the ABC model of anger, the A can also be called a _____.
16. In "The Fool in the Circle," who originally has more control over the situation?
17. True or false: One of the best ways we have of maintaining control over our lives is to be able to look at our perception of events.
18. True or false: Most people experience anger the same way.
19. List two direct triggers of your anger.
20. Match each of the following events with its place in the ABC model.

    a. You may have gotten your girlfriend or boyfriend mad at you.
    b. Without finding out if the statement is true, you confront both of them.
    c. Someone tells you that a girlfriend of yours has a secret date with your boyfriend.

ANSWERS: TEAM WORKSHEET 2

1. True.
2. Adrenaline.
3. True—You can learn to use these early signs of anger to begin to think and act in ways that will help you, such as deep breathing and relaxation.
4. d—Each of these emotions produces the flow of adrenaline in our body.
5. Cue.
6. Self-control.
7. b—Foods do not generally trigger behavior problems.
8. b—People who act impulsively, without thinking something through, are likely to get angrier.
9. False—Adrenaline, which is released in our bodies when we feel angry, helps to heighten our senses and to prepare us to either fight or flee when we are in danger.
10. Trigger.
11. b—Direct triggers are things other people do to you that make you angry. An indirect trigger is often a misperception of an event, or an incorrect idea of what is actually going on.
12. Various answers.
13. False—Getting extremely angry is a waste of personal power. By losing self-control, you lose control over the situation. There are ways of getting angry that will allow you to keep your sense of self-control.
14. a = antecedents, or events happening before you get angry.
    b = behaviors, or what you actually do when you get angry.
    c = consequences, or what happens as a result of your getting angry .
15. Trigger.
16. The fool, because it is the fool who is able to pull the student's strings and force the student into the circle.
17. True.
18. False.
19. Various answers.
20. A = antecedent event (c)
    B = behavior (b)
    C = consequence (a)

WEEK 3: COMMUNICATION SKILLS

Day 1: How People Communicate Without Talking

Focus: Explore how people use nonverbal communication in talking and listening.

Method: Demonstration; mini-lecture; exercise.

Time: One class period.

Capsule Description: This session is designed to help students become aware of nonverbal communication. Begin the session by asking a number of students to enter the room and portray, without talking, a particular emotion. A mini-lecture will follow. The session concludes with an exercise in which empathic listening skills are identified (Table 4.3), along with a list of listening techniques.

    1. Begin the session with role-playing: Ask individual students to enact specific emotions nonverbally. Ask them to enter the room and to show everyone, by their actions, what they are feeling. The rest of the class will guess what the emotion is and state what they observed that prompted the guess. Specific emotions such as anger, guilt, worry, and joy may be used.

    2. Using the above demonstration, the mini-lecture will cover how important nonverbal communication is in dealing with other people. Ask one student to portray *inconsistency* between verbal and nonverbal communication and ask the class which message they attend to. For instance, a student could act angry while saying he or she is not angry or could act sad while saying that he or she is not sad. The concept of nonverbal behavior on the part of the listener is introduced.

    3. Ask the class to break up into groups of three. In each group, two members will engage in listening and speaking while the third student notes what behaviors showed that the listener was really listening to the speaker. Before the roles are switched, the speaker also makes note of what the listener did that made him or her feel understood. Each segment will last about five minutes. At the end of the exercise, reconvene the class and ask them what they noted. Body language that indicates active listening may include using eye contact, some physical touching if appropriate, and leaning forward slightly toward the speaker. Other characteristics of active listening include putting aside one's own feelings for a moment, to allow the speaker to explore his or her own

TABLE 4.3   Listening Exercise

1. 5 minutes

    A observes.

    B and C talk together.

    B talks to C about one thing that was stressful today and how B coped with it.

2. 5 minutes

    B observes.

    A and C talk.

    C starts the talk.

    C talks to A about a recent situation in which C found it hard to listen to someone else.

3. 5 minutes

    C observes.

    A and B talk.

    A starts the talk.

    A talks to B about a situation in which someone did listen wholeheartedly to A.

Source: Adapted from Tubesing & Tubesing, 1984.

situation without being judged. End by suggesting that active listening can be summarized by a three-step process—*stop, look,* and *listen:*

- *Stop*—Stop talking or competing for attention and put aside your own thoughts and feelings for the moment. Take a deep breath if you need it to help you quiet down. Choose to focus on the speaker.
- *Look*—Look at the speaker and pay attention. Show interest by your verbal and nonverbal communication. Observe the speaker's feelings and nonverbal communication to help you to understand his or her situation.
- *Listen*—Really listen to the speaker. Listen to both words and body language. Listen to feelings as well as content. When speaking back, let the speaker know, without judging or criticizing, what it is you heard.

Day 2: Individual Rights and Empathic Listening

Focus: Explore the concept of individual rights in the context of communication skills and begin to reflect this knowledge in empathic listening.

Method: Discuss and reply to "Dear Auntie" letters.

Time: One class period.

Capsule Description: The class will generate a list of rights for themselves and then for others. Methods of voicing these rights will be discussed. Students will break up into small groups to develop answers to letters, which include the rights of the writers and of the people in their stories as well as a suggested response to the problem.

1. Begin by asking students to generate a list of their rights as individuals, things to which they feel they are entitled. This list may include such things as the right to be listened to, the right to have their own property, the right to explain their side of a story before a judgment is made, the right to remove themselves from situations that may hurt them in certain ways. Ask the class also to think of a list that defines the rights of others, including both peers and adults.

2. With both lists side by side on the chalkboard, ask the class to think of situations in which the rights of one side may be in conflict with those of the other side. For instance, individuals do have a right to be listened to, but if they let loose with a blast of out-of-control anger, they will violate the rights of those who have to listen to them. Not only will the listener be likely to feel worse, but the situation that made the listener angry is not likely to be solved.

3. Suggest that one way to bridge the gap between individual rights and the rights of others is to use empathic listening. Explain that by listening sensitively to others and letting them know that you understand them, you may meet your own needs without stepping on someone else's need.

Example: Mother to child: "Your room is a total disaster. I can't believe you can live in that filth. Get upstairs and clean it up now!"

Empathic response: "I know that you're upset about my room, but I just got back from school a few minutes ago, and I haven't had time to clean it up today." Point out that the mother has a right to expect a child to pitch in with housework, but that the child has a right to offer an explanation. Using an empathic response respects the rights of both parties.

4. Ask the class to break up into small groups. Distribute the "Dear Auntie" letters (Box 4.4). Each group will discuss each situation in terms of individual rights and develop a possible response. The response should help the writer see the situation in terms of his or her own rights as well as the rights of others. The response should also include possible empathic statements.

BOX 4.4

LETTERS: "DEAR AUNTIE"

Dear Auntie,
   Last week I went over to a friend's house and we started talking about sports. We were having an OK time until I mentioned that I liked the Tigers. My friend started acting weird and kept trying to convince me that this other team was better. My friend kept saying that I did not really understand or I wouldn't feel the way I did. Every time I tried to talk, my friend interrupted and kept talking about that other team. I wish there was something I could have done to make it different because my friend and I haven't talked since. What could I have done?

Confused

Dear Auntie,
   There is a situation at my house that drives me crazy. It's my little brother—he's always into my stuff and he won't leave it alone even when I close my door. In fact, the more I close my door to him, the more he seems to try and get in. I often end up screaming at him to leave me alone and then he cries, and I feel terrible. What can I do?

Helpless

Dear Auntie,
   My cousin came over to spend the week with us while his parents are away. The problem is that we don't like any of the same TV shows. If I'm watching my favorite show, he'll come in and say, "That show is for babies," and turn the channel. I get mad, but I know he's a guest and I should try and make him welcome. The problem is, I'm getting to the point where I'm getting pretty angry with all this. What should I do?

Angry

Day 3: Assertiveness Training; Assertiveness Techniques

Focus: Define *assertiveness* and practice methods of assertiveness.

Method: Discussion; lecture, role-playing.

Time: One class period.

Capsule Description: This session is designed to define and to explore different methods of assertiveness. It begins with the teacher leading a discussion on how students now attempt to assert their own rights. Definitions and new techniques are included in the discussion. A role-playing activity will follow that gives students a chance to practice new responses.

1. The teacher will ask the class what they now do when someone violates their rights. Ask them what they do when someone cuts in front of them in line. Pass out the "Assertiveness Information Sheet" and ask them to identify their own current style. Suggest that using the passive approach may avoid problems but leave you feeling powerless and exploited. The aggressive style often leads to hostility and to fighting. The assertive style does not guarantee that you will get what you want, but you can ask for it sometimes in such a way that you feel good about yourself without trampling on the rights of others.

2. Review "Assertiveness Techniques," following the information sheet, and ask the class to think of different ways they could handle their own situation.

3. Pass out the scenes for role-playing (Box 4.5) and ask the students to break up into small groups. Before enacting these scenes, the group should discuss what the primary right of each participant in the scene is and which assertiveness technique would be most effective. While in these small groups the students will enact the various responses.

ASSERTIVENESS INFORMATION SHEET

Interpersonal Styles

The first step in assertiveness training is to identify three basic styles of interpersonal behavior.

Aggressive style. Typical examples of aggressive behavior are fighting, accusing, threatening, and generally stepping on people without regard for their feelings. The advantage of this kind of behavior is that people do not push the aggressive person around. The disadvantage is that people do not want to be around him or her.

Passive style. People are behaving passively when they let others push them around, when they do not stand up for themselves, and when they do what they are told, regardless of how they feel about it. The advantage of being passive is that you rarely experience direct rejection. The disadvantage is that you are taken advantage of, and you store up a heavy burden of resentment and anger.

Assertive style. People are behaving assertively when they stand up for themselves, express their true feelings, and do not let others take advantage of them. At the same time, they are considerate of others' feelings. The advantage of being assertive is that you get what you want, usually without making others mad. If you are assertive, you can act in your own best interest and not feel guilty or wrong about it. Meekness and withdrawal, attack and blame are no longer needed when assertive behavior is mastered. They are seen for what they are— sadly inadequate strategies of escape that create more pain and stress than they prevent. Before you achieve assertive behavior, you must really face the fact that the passive and aggressive styles have often failed to get you what you want.

ASSERTIVENESS TECHNIQUES

"Broken record." This response involves a calm repetition of what you want ("Please give me back my radio."). There is no change in voice tone or tempo; just keep asking calmly for what you want.

"How to say NO." Saying no when you need to can prevent the buildup of anger and resentment that may later result in an outburst. When you say "NO," be firm and clear. The answer should be short and to the point. Don't be overly apologetic, but if you need to, provide the person with another course of action. ("No, I can't help you clean up your garage today. I have other things that my parents asked me to do. Maybe you could get your sister to help.")

"Empathic assertion." This involves listening sensitively to a speaker's feelings, and it can be very useful when dealing with authority figures. It is very similar to the empathic responses we practiced yester-day. (Teacher: "What are you doing in the hallway? Get to class now or you'll be in detention." Student: "I can tell you're mad because you think I'm trying to cut class, but I was having a conference with my last teacher and he wrote this hall pass for me.")

BOX 4.5

ASSERTIVENESS: SCENES FOR ROLE-PLAYING

1. A friend borrowed $10 three weeks ago and hasn't paid you back yet.

   Your primary right is _____.
   Your friend's primary right is _____.
   A good assertiveness technique to use here is ____.

2. A friend borrowed a tape and returned it to you damaged.

   Your primary right is _____.
   Your friend's primary right is _____.
   A good assertiveness technique to use here is ____.

3. You go to the store to return a sale item you bought, which is defective.

   Your primary right is _____.
   The clerk's or the store's primary right is _____.
   A good assertiveness technique to use here is ____.

4. Your aunt is trying to set you up on a blind date with the child of her out-of-town friend.

   Your primary right is _____.
   Your aunt's primary right is _____.
   The friend's child's primary right is _____.
   A good assertiveness technique to use here is ____.

5. You go to a restaurant and order fish, but it comes out overdone and tasteless.

   Your primary right is _____.
   The waiter's or waitress's primary right is _____.
   A good assertiveness technique to use here is ____.

TEAM WORKSHEET 3

1. True or false: Talking is the only way people communicate.
2. True or false: Sometimes people who look angry and aggressive are really scared.
3. After an angry outburst, the *least* likely outcome will be that

   a. you'll feel a lot better
   b. you'll feel guilty
   c. people will learn to listen more closely to you in the future

4. True or false: A friend who always talks to you about what makes him or her angry probably feels better and does a better job of dealing with anger than a friend who doesn't always talk to you.
5. Which of these behaviors would be considered aggressive?

   a. teasing
   b. arguing
   c. threatening
   d. all of the above
   e. none of the above

6. True or false: An angry outburst may be caused by not knowing how else to act.
7. _____ is defined as expressing your needs clearly and firmly without hurting someone else.
8. _____ is expressing your needs at someone else's expense.
9. True or false: A person who is just quietly listening to you is communicating.
10. What behavior is *not* included in active listening?

    a. eye contact
    b. summary statements
    c. paying attention to what is going on around you
    d. listening for the speaker's feelings

11. True or false: After you vent your anger in a loud and forceful way, you feel much better, so it's obviously the right thing to do.
12. Unscramble this word: RESTASIVE.
13. The assertion technique that involves a calm repetition of what you want is called the "_____."
14. True or false: Keeping anger in can hurt you, so it is important always to express yourself fully.

15. True or false: When learning how to say no to someone, you should always be really apologetic.
16. A form of assertion that involves listening to a speaker's feelings is called "_____."
17. True or false: How we learn to communicate contributes to the stress we feel in our lives.
18. Match each word with its definition.

    1. Passive   a. standing up for your rights but at the same time respecting the rights of others

    2. Assertive   b. demanding your rights with no regard for the other person's rights

    3. Aggressive   c. letting someone take away your rights

19. True or false: By being assertive, we can always get what we want.
20. True or false: Active listening is hard work and takes energy.

ANSWERS: TEAM WORKSHEET 3

1. False.
2. True—Many emotionally charged situations give us similar feelings. If we label every feeling "anger," even if it's not, we will probably act angry.
3. c—Some people feel good after they blow up and some people don't, but if you blow up a lot people will be more likely to learn to avoid you than to listen to you.
4. False—Talking can help us feel understood and cared about, but it does not make anger go away. A great deal of talking may even maintain your anger instead of making it go away.
5. d.
6. True—At times people express anger because they don't know how else to act in a situation.
7. Assertiveness.
8. Aggressiveness.
9. True—People who really know how to listen can let us know, without saying a word, that they are interested in us and that they care what happens to us.
10. c.
11. False—You may feel a lot better, but the people around you may feel worse and the problem may remain unsolved.
12. Assertive.
13. "Broken record."
14. False—The idea that holding in your anger can "clog your emotional arteries" ignores the fact that other people's rights and feelings are involved. If your angry outburst causes someone to punch you out and you end up in the hospital, it won't matter that your emotional arteries are unclogged.
15. False—Saying no should be done in a firm, specific, honest manner, without being overly apologetic.
16. "Empathic assertion."
17. True—Much of the stress we feel is the result of interpersonal friction. How we communicate with others may reduce stress if we communicate in a way that permits solutions.
18. 1-c, 2-a, 3-b.
19. False—We may not always get what we want but we can at least know we acted in a way we can earn respect for ourselves.
20. True.

WEEK 4: SELF-INSTRUCTION TRAINING

Day 1: Self-Statements and Stages of Confrontation

Focus: Define self-statements and identify various self-statements useful for the different stages of a confrontation.

Method: Demonstration; mini-lecture; small groups.

Time: One class period.

Capsule Description: The opening demonstration—the "nine dots" exercise—is designed to show students how learning to think differently can lead to new solutions. The mini-lecture will define *self-statements* and suggest certain helpful ones for different stages of confrontation. The class will break up into small groups and brainstorm further self-statements.

1. Begin the session with the "nine dots" exercise. Draw the nine dots on the board and ask the class to draw a figure just like that on a sheet of paper. Tell them that their task is to connect all nine dots by drawing four straight continuous lines (without lifting the pencil or retracing lines). If any students solve the problem, ask them to show their solution on the board; if not, show students the solution (Figure 4.1).

Ask the students about the impact of the square—did it affect their ability to solve the problem? It is hard to break out of the mental impulse of trying to go around the square with four lines and leave the middle dot untouched. How must students think in order to be able to solve the puzzle? They need to break out of their mental habits and mental images. What effect might this idea have on their ability to manage difficult situations?

2. The mini-lecture will introduce the concept of *self-statements* as things we say to ourselves to remind us to act in a certain way or to believe something. Show how our minds can change our emotions by describing this situation: A father has just criticized his son, and the son begins to think how unfair it was. How would the son feel? (Angry.) If, moments later, the son began to think that maybe his father is really disappointed in him and that maybe the father doesn't love him the way he used to, how would the son then feel? (Sad.) Briefly, discuss the concept of *perspective*—taking it as a tool to use. With this tool, students can learn to remind themselves to step back and look at and think about a problem differently.

3. Introduce the idea of *stages of confrontation* by writing the four stages on the board:

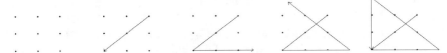

FIGURE 4.1   The "nine-dots" exercise.

- Stage 1: Preparing for conflict
- Stage 2: Confrontation
- Stage 3: Coping with arousal
- Stage 4: Reflection and evaluation

Under each stage, write an adaptive thought and a maladaptive thought and ask students how these thoughts would change the person's behavior. For example:

- Stage 1: "I know I can handle this" versus "This kid is going to make me look like a fool."
- Stage 2: "I will stay calm" versus "I'm going to blow this kid away."
- Stage 3: "I'll just relax and breathe deeply" versus "I feel really angry, and I'm going to let this kid have it."
- Stage 4: "I did that pretty well" versus "I can't believe I went out of control again."
  or: "I know these new things take time to learn, so I'll try again" versus "This stuff doesn't work . . . Just forget it!"

4. Ask the students to put each statement on the second handout (Box 4.6) into the appropriate stage of a confrontation. Give students a copy that does *not* show the stage numbers after each statement. (The stages of conflict and confrontation are adapted from Feindler & Ecton, 1986.)

Day 2: Self-Statements and Belief Systems

Focus: Define and explore personal belief systems and their effect on behaviors.

Method: Mini-lecture; small group exercise.

Time: One class period.

Capsule Description: A mini-lecture will introduce the concept of belief systems. Following this, the class will break up into small groups to work on the handout.

BOX 4.6

HANDOUT: ADAPTIVE THOUGHTS FOR STAGES OF CONFLICT AND CONFRONTATION

I'll be able to handle this. . . . I'm ready. (1)

I handled that well! (4)

I feel my heart pumping—time to slow down. (3)

I'll just stay calm; there's no point in blowing up. (2)

I'll just think of what I need to do. (2)

I did my best, and even if it didn't get solved I won't continue to be upset. (4)

This may be hard, but I'm ready and I know how to deal with it. (1)

I'm feeling very tense. I need to calm down. (3)

There's no way that kid will do what he says. I'll just ignore him. (2)

I'm feeling angry. . . . What's getting to me? (3)

I worked out a way to handle this. I know what to do. (1)

I actually got through that without getting angry. I could've been upset but I wasn't. (4)

I handled that well. (4)

Well, it didn't go quite the way I had planned, but some things will be harder than others. (4)

This may be hard, but I know I can do it. (1)

As long as I stay calm, I'm in control of the situation. (2)

That kid is threatening me again. What should I say to him? (1)

I don't need to prove myself. I'm not going to make more of this than I need to. (2)

I've got to remember that I used to lose control completely, and now I'm in much better control (4).

1. Present the concept of belief systems to the class as a series of self-statements upon which we act without thinking. Certain belief systems may be labeled as the "super" syndrome, the "workaholic" syndrome, the "striving" syndrome, and the "tough" syndrome (Tubesing & Tubesing, 1984). Examples of self-statements which reflect these syndromes are "I must always be the best," "I must work harder than anyone else," "I can always do better," "I don't care what others think of me." Ask the class to come up with other examples.

2. Have the groups come up with more helpful self-statements in each case.

HANDOUT: SYNDROMES IN BELIEF SYSTEMS

1. *"Super" Syndrome*

    "I always have to be the best."
    "I can always do better than everyone else."

    A situation where these beliefs could make you mad: _____
    A more helpful set of self-statements would be: _____

2. *"Workalcoholic" Syndrome*

    "I must work harder than everyone else all the time."
    "I'm worth only as much as I accomplish."

    A situation where these beliefs could make you mad:_____
    A more helpful set of self-statements would be: _____

3. *"Striving" Syndrome*

    "I must always try harder."
    "No matter what I've done, I could have done better."

    A situation where these beliefs could make you mad: _____
    A more helpful set of self-statements would be: _____

4. *"Tough" Syndrome*

    "I don't show it when I'm hurt."
    "I don't need anyone else."

    A situation where these beliefs could make you mad: _____
    A more helpful set of self-statements would be: _____

Day 3: The Importance of Self-Reinforcement

Focus: Discuss and explore self-reinforcement.

Method: Develop individual lists of pleasurable activities and work on applications in small groups.

Time: One class period.

Capsule Description: Students will complete the "Pleasant Events Inventory" (Wodarski & Wodarski, 1993) to gain some awareness of how they can reinforce themselves. The small group activity allows students the chance to practice new skills learned this week.

    1. Pass out the following Pleasant Events Inventory, explaining that we need to know how to reward ourselves by thinking we are OK, as well as by treating ourselves as though we are OK. Have the students (individually) circle the items they would find pleasurable, adding any of their own not on the list. Tell them that they now have a list of things they can use as rewards for themselves when they have worked hard on their new behavior.

    2. Ask the class to break up into their small groups. Pass out the "Anger-Provoking Situations" handout and have each group complete it.

HANDOUT 1: PLEASANT EVENTS INVENTORY

Name _____ Date_____

Directions: Circle each item you would find pleasurable.

1. Meeting someone new of the same sex
2. Playing baseball or softball
3. Buying things for myself
4. Going to a sports event
5. Pleasing my parents
6. Watching TV
7. Laughing
8. Solving a problem or cross-word puzzle
9. Thinking about myself or my problems
10. Going to a party
11. Being with friends
12. Wearing new clothes
13. Dancing
14. Dating, courting, etc.
15. Playing in a sports competition
16. Going on outings (picnic, park)
17. Helping someone
18. Meeting someone new of the opposite sex
19. Going to a drive-in
20. Talking on the telephone
21. Having daydreams
22. Kissing
23. Doing a project in my own way
24. Giving a party
25. Going to a restaurant
26. Visiting friends
27. Talking with people in class
28. Being relaxed
29. Reading the newspaper
30. Running, jogging, exercise
31. Listening to music
32. Talking about sex
33. Reading magazines
34. Shopping
35. Bicycling
36. Staying up late

Other Activities

_____

_____

_____

HANDOUT 2: ANGER-PROVOKING SITUATIONS

1. Jeff was called on in class but didn't know the answer. He thought he heard someone giggle. After class, a couple of people teased him about it.

   a. Jeff's positive self-statement: It's OK to fail sometimes.
   b. Jeff's negative self-statement: I can't stand it when this happens, and it's awful to look stupid in front of people and have them tease me. Possible belief system behind this self-statement. _____
   c. Finish the story both ways. Include further self-statements and self-evaluations, as well as probable behaviors.

2. Beth heard her best friend invite someone else to go shopping. Beth wondered why her friend wasn't asking her. After all, they did everything together.

   a. Beth's positive self-statement: I can handle this. I know how to assert my feelings without hurting my friend. After all, I was thinking I wanted to spend more time doing something else anyhow.
   b. Beth's negative self-statement: I can't believe she's doing this to me. How awful! Well, I won't let her know how this hurts me. I'll just ignore her and let her see how it feels. Possible belief system behind this self-statement: _____
   c. Finish the story both ways. Include further self-statements and self-evaluations as well as behaviors.

3. John was used to being the best on his volleyball team, and he was very proud of this. In one game he was having an off day and the members of the other team kept teasing and yelling at him about how bad he was.

   a. John's positive self-statement: It's OK for me to have an off day. I remember plenty of days where I was really good.
   b. John's negative self-statement: It's terrible that I'm not the best and that everyone knows it. Possible belief system behind this self-statement: _____
   c. Finish the story both ways. Include further self-statements and self-evaluations as well as any behaviors.

TEAM WORKSHEET 4

1. True or false: We can change how we feel by changing how we think.
2. True or false: The same event will always produce the same feelings in all people.
3. If Joe believes that he must always be the best at anything he tries, how may he react to striking out at a baseball game?
4. If Jane believes that she always does her best and that she is OK no matter what happens, how may she react to striking out at a baseball game?
5. Give two examples of positive self-statements.
6. Give two examples of negative self-statements.
7. True or false: Self-statements are strongly ingrained and impossible to change.
8. Name three things you can do to help yourself to feel better if you find out that your friend didn't invite you to a party.
9. What could you say to yourself if you feel yourself starting to become angry?
10. What could you say to yourself if you are not successful in avoiding conflict?
11. What could you say to yourself after handling a problem situation and resolving the conflict?
12. True or false: One way to help ourselves learn a new skill is to give ourselves feedback after we try it.
13. Unscramble these words: PECTRISPEEV-KATING
14. True or false: People who are aggressive often see a threat where none exists.
15. How we feel and how we act are determined by:

    a. How other people behave toward us
    b. Our thoughts about what is happening to us
    c. The picture we form in our minds about what is happening to us
    d. b and c

16. Match these self-statements with the stages of confrontation.
    (1) I handled that well.   (a) Preparing for conflict
    (2) My heart is pounding. . . .   (b) Reflection and
        I'll start my deep breathing.   evaluation
    (3) I know how to do this.   (c) Coping with arousal
        I'm prepared.   (d) Confrontation
    (4) I'm in control of myself.

17. True or false: It is possible to learn to control your body's physical responses with your mind.
18. True or false: Anger is simply a biological reflex, and it is very similar in animals and humans.
19. What are the first two stages of an angry confrontation?
20. What are the last two stages of an angry confrontation?

ANSWERS: TEAM WORKSHEET 4

1. True.
2. False—Different beliefs will produce different feelings.
3. He may become very angry at himself or at others.
4. She is likely to accept it and go on with her day.
5. Various answers.
6. Various answers.
7. False—By learning to identify and become aware of self-statements, we can begin to change them.
8. Various answers. (Examples: go shopping, spend time with a friend, go for a walk, listen to music, help someone else.)
9. This could be rough, but I know how to handle this without getting angry. I can be assertive without being aggressive.
10. I'll forget about this because thinking about it only makes me angrier. I won't take this too personally, and it's probably not that serious.
11. I handled that really well. I could've gotten upset, but I didn't—I did a good job.
12. True.
13. Perspective-taking.
14. True.
15. d.
16. 1—b; 2—c; 3—a; 4—d
17. True—We can control how fast and how deeply we breathe, and even our heart rate, by mentally concentrating on these things.
18. False—The actual physical response may be similar, but humans are angered by memories and can hold onto their anger for years—far longer than the situation that prompted the anger.
19. Prepare for conflict; confrontation.
20. Coping with arousal; reflection and evaluation.

WEEK 5: PROBLEM SOLVING

Day 1: Defining Positive and Negative Methods of Coping

Focus: Define and explore both positive and negative coping, with an emphasis on consequences of each.

Method: Mini-lecture; small group exercise.

Time: One class period.

Capsule Description: The mini-lecture will cover the difference between positive and negative coping. The class will then break up into small groups and brainstorm their own list of coping methods and the possible consequences of using each one.

    1. Begin the session by defining a *coping mechanism* as a method we use for dealing with stress and anger. We all have different coping mechanisms, and every one of us has coping methods that work—if they didn't work, we wouldn't keep using them. The problem with some coping methods is that while they may help us reduce our stress or anger initially, the long-term consequences of using them may be negative. For instance, angry people may swear loudly and hit other people in order to express and reduce their anger. This may initially communicate anger and stop the others from doing whatever they were doing to make you angry, but the long-term effects may be very serious. People may learn to avoid a violent person. Also, using violence often prompts violence in return, and you may be hurt. In addition, the use of violence often prompts authority figures or the police to step in. Obviously, this negative coping method may be very effective in the short run for dealing with anger-provoking situations, but in the long run the cost of this behavior is very high. Positive coping methods will relieve stress without hurting anyone—yourself or someone else.

    2. Pass out the following handout of positive and negative coping methods. Have the class look it over before breaking up into groups to see if there are any additional coping methods they would like to add to the list.

    3. Have the class break up into small groups and brainstorm the long-term and short-term effects of using the different coping methods.

HANDOUT: POSITIVE AND NEGATIVE COPING

Negative Coping	Positive Coping
Using drugs and alcohol	Looking for the humor in a situation
Pretending that nothing is wrong	Exercising
Using aggression or violence	Eating healthful foods
Always imagining the worst thing that can happen	Using relaxation
	Using positive self-statements for coping
Going on a spending spree	Using assertiveness
Bingeing on food	Playing music or an instrument
Getting even, getting revenge	Playing a game
Demanding your own way	Relabeling and changing your perspective
Complaining	Sharing your feelings in a way that won't hurt others

Day 2: Methods of Dealing With Anger-Provoking Situations

Focus: Explore alternative methods of dealing with anger.

Method: Mini-lecture; small group exercise.

Time: One class period.

Capsule Description: A mini-lecture will be presented, covering three different methods of dealing with problems: (1) alter them, (2) avoid them, or (3) accept them. The class will break up into small groups and complete the handout, which asks them to come up with examples of methods for a problem situation. The groups will share their ideas with each other.

1. Begin the lecture by discussing the three methods listed above, the "three A's." All three can be effective, but the problem is knowing which one may work the best in a given situation. Illustrate each method with examples. People can *alter* a problem by changing it through assertiveness and communication skills. People can *avoid* a problem by walking away, saying "no," knowing what will be a problem, and avoiding the circumstance. People can *accept* problems by changing their perception with appropriate self-statements.
2. Have the class break into small groups and fill out the handout.
3. Have the class reconvene and share their responses to the handout. (Taken from Tubesing & Tubesing, 1984.)

HANDOUT

Scene 1

You have a new teacher at school who doesn't seem to like you. No matter what you do, he or she always seems to criticize you or to single you out from the group as the one with the problem. What can you do?

    Alter it: _____   Avoid it: _____   Accept it: _____

Scene 2

Your friend seems to be avoiding you. You are getting mad because you think that your friend is trying to ditch you and join another group of kids. What could you do?

    Alter it: _____   Avoid it: _____   Accept it: _____

Day 3: Problem Solving

Focus: Learn and apply the problem-solving method.

Method: Mini-lecture; small group exercise.

Time: One class period.

Capsule Description: The mini-lecture will cover the stages in problem solving and give the class an example of the process. The small group exercise will ask students to use the process on their own.

1. Begin the lecture by listing the six steps in problem solving.

- *Step 1:* State the problem. The emphasis here is on stating the problem in a manner that will allow it to be solved. For instance, a problem statement such as "My parents are mean" does not help us to solve the problem. But the statement: "I need to do something about the fights I have with my parents" suggests that different alternatives are possible.
- *Step 2:* Identify your own needs as well as the needs of others involved. This will help ensure that you accept the situation in a way that does not hurt others as you help yourself.
- *Step 3:* Brainstorm different alternatives, coping methods, assertiveness skills, and communication skills that may help. It is useful to remember the "three A's" of problem management used yesterday. A very important step in this process is to allow any alternative to be listed, even if at first it seems silly. Silly ideas may include important points, which can end up helping you.
- *Step 4:* List the pros and cons of each alternative. This is easily done by using a plus sign (+) for each pro and a minus sign (–) for each con.
- *Step 5:* Pick an alternative to try. To see which alternative is most promising, it is easy to go back and sum up the positive and negative signs.
- *Step 6:* Evaluate your attempted solution. If that solution didn't work, go back to your list and try the next most likely alternative.

2. Write a problem on the board and lead the class in an example of the problem-solving process.

3. Have the class break into small groups and try out the process on one or more of the examples provided in the following handout.

HANDOUT: PROBLEM SOLVING

Problem 1

You are at the store shopping for some last-minute Christmas gifts for your friends and family. The store is very crowded, and people seem to be tense. You have finally found what you want, and as you walk up to the checkout counter an older woman rushes past you, knocking your gifts out of your arms and cutting in front of you in line.

Problem 2

Your dad is on your back about something all the time. He doesn't like your friends, so he won't let you hang out with them. But he also says he won't pick your friends for you.

Problem 3

You and your sister are always fighting over the bathroom you share. Not only does she hog the bathroom in the morning when you both have to get to school, but she leaves it filthy. You're fed up with the situation, and it seems as though you're angry with her all day.

TEAM WORKSHEET 5

1. True or false: Anger can help us to solve problems.
2. Describe two ways in which anger can be expressed positively or neutrally rather than aggressively.
3. True or false: It is best to talk about our anger to anyone who will listen.
4. The first step in problem solving is to _____.
5. True or false: Once you pick out a solution to try, you should stand by it.
6. When you are brainstorming in a group, it is important not to _____ any of the possible solutions offered.
7. True or false: The problem-solving approach can also be used by your family in deciding who gets to use the car at what times.
8. If a solution you decide to try is not working, what should you do?
9. Name the "three A's" of dealing with problems.
10. Name two negative coping mechanisms.
11. Name two positive coping mechanisms.
12. How many alternatives should you use in problem solving?
13. True or false: Problem solving doesn't really work with big problems.
14. Name all six steps in the problem-solving process, in order.
15. Name three situations in which problem solving may be helpful.
16. True or false: For any problem, there is only one right answer.
17. After stating a problem, it is important to _____ _____ _____ of all who are involved.
18. True or false: The brainstorming process in problem solving must be done in a group.
19. True or false: In brainstorming, silly ideas are not evaluated.
20. True or false: There is no perfect solution to each problem.

Source: Wodarski, 1986a.

ANSWERS: TEAM WORKSHEET 5

1. True—Anger can act as a cue that we need to do something, but it is up to us to decide what is the best course of action.
2. Numerous answers are acceptable. Examples: Running around a track very fast; playing the guitar hard and loud.
3. False—It may be OK to initially express our anger in an assertive manner, but continually talking about anger can maintain the angry feeling.
4. State the problem in concrete terms.
5. False—Effective problem solvers are always reevaluating their decisions.
6. Evaluate or criticize.
7. True.
8. Go back to your list of possible solutions and pick another one.
9. Alter it, avoid it, or accept it.
10. Various answers are acceptable. Examples: smoking, shouting.
11. Various answers are acceptable. Examples: problem solving, exercise.
12. As many as you can think of.
13. False.
14. (1) State the problem. (2) Identify needs. (3) Brainstorm. (4) List pros and cons. (5) Pick an alternative. (6) Evaluate the outcome.
15. Various answers are acceptable.
16. False.
17. Identify the needs.
18. False.
19. False.
20. True.

WEEK 6: WRAP-UP

Day 1: Predicting a Relapse

Focus: Identify problematic future situations that students may be unable to handle successfully.

Method: Mini-lecture; small groups; role-playing with participation by the class.

Time: One class period.

Capsule Description: The mini-lecture will provide some background on the normality of setbacks and provide some groundwork for coping with them. After the lecture, the class will break up into small groups, and each group will develop its own role-playing situation of a possible failure. Each group will perform its short enactment, and the class will give feedback afterward. Feedback will consist of appropriate self-statements and skills to be used.

     1. The mini-lecture will begin by "normalizing" setbacks. The problem is not so much the occasional failure as our response to it. People often give up after failing once, thinking, "I'm not able to do this. I'll just give up." Any new skill we try to learn will not be instantly successful. Think of any other skill you learned, like riding a bike. People are not able to climb up onto a bike seat and do wheelies the first time they try. Another thing that may happen to you when you first begin to try out your new behaviors is that the people who are used to seeing you get angry may actually try harder to provoke you if you don't get angry right away. Think of what happens when you put your money into a vending machine but don't get your snack. You may try putting in more money, and if that doesn't work, you may begin to shake the machine or to kick it to get it to do what you expect it to do. Another example may be coming home from school and expecting your mom to be there, the way she always is. If she doesn't answer right away, you will probably yell louder. You will initially try harder to get her to do what she normally does—answer you or explain why she wasn't where she usually is. You probably won't immediately think that she has changed her schedule or her habits.

     2. With these two main points in mind—self-evaluation and the response of others—have the class break up into small groups and develop their own short role-playing situations.

3. Have each group perform. When the group is finished role-playing, have the class brainstorm appropriate self-talk and coping strategies for each situation.

Days 2 and 3: Wrap Up and Develop a Videotape Presentation

Focus: Help students to pull the various segments together into a meaningful whole.

Method: Small groups will develop a video presentation.

Time: Two class periods.

Capsule Description: Small groups will spend two class periods developing a video designed to "sell" to other students the program for reducing and controlling anger. The video is a sales device, so the groups should be encouraged to develop theme songs and slogans as well as to point out the advantages of the program. Although it is not mandatory, actual videotaping of each group presentation may enhance the exercise.

Day 4: Presenting Videos

Focus: Allow students to see other groups' video presentations.

Method: Video presentation and discussion.

Time: One class period.

Capsule Description: Class will view the video presentations. A discussion will follow, which will cover the following points:

1. What was one thing all the presentations had in common—any major themes that emerged, or any techniques or learning that seemed to be most important to the class.
2. What was the strongest selling point of each video? Did the focus on advantages of using the program, or perhaps the emphasis on a particular technique, seem stronger?
3. How did the videos help you to pull things together?
4. How did the videos help you know how to use what you've learned now that the program is done?

5. What was the most important thing you learned from the program?

Day 5: Pretest and Posttest

Directions: Administer pretest/posttest.

1. True or false: Our lives would be much better if we had no stress at all.
2. The way you _____ others can change the amount of stress you feel in a certain situation.

   a. think about
   b. behave toward
   c. talk with
   d. all of the above

3. True or false: There is a strong connection between the amount of stress a person is under and how much anger he or she is likely to experience.
4. True or false: The more we feel in control of a situation, the less likely we are to feel angry or stressed out over it.
5. True or false: Whenever people get really angry, they will act aggressively.
6. True or false: Anger is a bad emotion, and we should try not to feel it.
7. One function of anger is to _____.
8. Which situation will be likely to produce stress?

   a. Something good, like your family moving to a nice home where you finally have you own room.
   b. Something bad, like your favorite teacher leaving in midsemester and being replaced by a new, very stern teacher.
   c. a and b

9. Anger releases in our bodies a hormone called _____.
10. The signal your body sends to you that you are becoming angry is called a/an _____.
11. Which student will most likely act angrier?

    a. One who thinks a long time about why he or she is angry and what to do about it.
    b. One who acts without thinking about it.

12. An event that provokes anger is called a/an _____.

13. An example of an indirect trigger is

    a. someone cutting in front of you when you're in line.
    b. thinking that the teacher put you on detention because he or she hates you, when in fact it was because you broke a rule.

14. What are the three steps in the ABC model of looking at anger?

15. True or false: One of the best ways we have of maintaining control over our lives is to be able to look at our perceptions of events.

16. List two direct triggers of your anger.

17. True or false: Talking is the only way people communicate.

18. After an angry outburst, the *least* likely outcome will be

    a. You'll feel a lot better.
    b. You'll feel guilty.
    c. People will listen more closely to you next time.

19. Which of these behaviors would be considered aggressive?

    a. teasing
    b. arguing
    c. threatening
    d. all of the above
    e. none of the above

20. _____ is defined as expressing your own needs clearly and firmly without hurting someone else.

21. _____ is expressing your own needs at someone else's expense.

22. What behavior is *not* included in active listening?

    a. eye contact
    b. summary statements
    c. paying attention to what's going on around you
    d. listening for the speaker's feelings

23. The assertion technique that involves a calm repetition of what you want is called "_____."

24. True or false: By being assertive, we can always get what we want.

25. True or false: We can change how we feel by changing how we think.

26. If Joe believes that he must always be the best at anything he tries, how may he react to striking out at a baseball game?

27. Give two examples of positive self-statements.
28. Give two example of negative self-statements.
29. What can you say to yourself if you feel yourself starting to become angry?
30. Match these statements with the stages of confrontation.

    1. I handled that well.   a. preparing for conflict
    2. My heart is pounding. . . .   b. confrontation
       I'll start my breathing.   c. coping with arousal
    3. I know how to do this.   d. reflection and evaluation
       I'm prepared.
    4. I'm in control of myself.

31. Describe two ways in which anger can be expressed positively or neutrally rather than aggressively.
32. The first step in problem solving is to _____.
33. True or false: Once you pick out a solution to try, you should stand by it.
34. When you are brainstorming in a group, it is important not to _____ any of the possible solutions.
35. Name the "three A's" of dealing with problems.
36. Name two negative coping mechanisms.
37. Name two positive coping mechanisms.
38. Name all six steps in the problem-solving process, in order. (Additional items will be added from relaxation unit)

ANSWERS TO PRETEST AND POSTTEST

1. False
2. d
3. True
4. True
5. False
6. False
7. Various answers
8. c
9. Adrenaline
10. Cue
11. b
12. Trigger
13. b
14. A = antecedent
    B = behavior
    C = consequences
15. True
16. Various answers
17. False
18. c
19. d
20. Assertiveness
21. Aggressiveness
22. c
23. Broken record
24. False
25. True
26. He may become angry with himself.
27. Various answers
28. Various answers
29. Various answers
30. 1—d; 2—b; 3—a; 4—d.
31. Various answers
32. State the problem in concrete terms.
33. False
34. Evaluate or criticize
35. Alter it; avoid it: or accept it.
36. Various answers
37. Various answers
38. (1) State the problem; (2) identify needs; (3) brainstorm; (4) list pros and cons; (5) pick an alternative; (6) evaluate the attempted solutions.

REFERENCES

Boldizar, J. P., Perry, D. G., & Perry, L. C. (1989). Outcome values and aggression. *Child Development, 60,* 571–579.

Feindler, E. L., & Ecton, R. B. (1986). *Adolescent anger control: Cognitive behavioral techniques.* New York: Pergamon.

Feindler, E. L., Marriot, S. A., & Iwata, M. (1984). Group anger control training for junior high school delinquents. *Cognitive Therapy and Research, 8,* 299–311.

Hains, A. A., & Szyjakowski, M. (1990). A cognitive stress-reduction intervention program for adolescents. *Journal of Counseling Psychology, 37,* 79–84.

Larson, J. D. (1992). Anger and aggression management techniques through the Think First curriculum. *Journal of Rehabilitation, 18(1–2),* 101–117.

Meichenbaum, D., & Cameron, R. (1983). Stress inoculation training. In D. Meichenbaum and M. E. Jarenko (Eds.), *Stress reduction and prevention,* 115–154. New York: Plenum.

Novaco, R. W. (1975). *Anger control.* Lexington, MA: Lexington.

Rapp, L., & Wodarski, J. (in press). Juvenile violence: Its high risk factors, current interventions, and implications for social work practice. *Journal of Applied Social Sciences.*

Tavris, C. (1982). *Anger: The misunderstood emotion.* New York: Simon & Schuster.

Tubesing, N. L., & Tubesing, B. A. (Eds.). (1984). *Structured exercises in stress management,* Vols. 1–3. Duluth, MN: Whole Person.

Wodarski, J. S. (1986). Depression and suicide prevention by the teams-games-tournaments method. (Unpublished manual.) Athens: University of Georgia School of Social Work.

Wodarski, J. S., & Hedrick, M. (1987). Violent children: A practice paradigm. *Social Work in Education, 10,* 28–42.

Wodarski, J. S., & Wodarski, L. A. (1993). *Curriculums and practical aspects of implementation: Preventive health services for adolescents.* Lanham, MD: University Press of America, Inc.

Chapter 5

Curriculum for Parents

INTRODUCTION

As the participants arrive, greet them and introduce them to each other. When all the participants are present, explain that they have a common bond: they are parents of a violent adolescent, or they want to learn to prevent anger or violence in their children.

Explain the format and subject matter of the sessions to be conducted.

1. Stress the importance of confidentiality.
2. Explain the importance of beginning sessions on time and of regular attendance. Qualify that sessions will consist of three-hour sessions each week for seven weeks.
3. Give participants pretest.
4. Discuss material that will be presented in each section.

WEEK 1: DEFINE AND EXPLORE THE PROBLEM

What Is Anger?

Focus: Define anger and its uses.

Method: Mini-lecture; discussion.

Capsule Description: This exercise is designed to help parents to define anger and to see that it can be expressed in different ways by different people and it can be a useful emotion.

   1. A mini-lecture is presented, explaining that while anger is felt by all people, it will be expressed differently depending on cultural learning. Help the group to recognize the difference between anger and aggression. Define both concepts. *Anger* is a hostile feeling. *Aggression* is hostile behavior aimed at another person. The key distinction is that anger is a feeling whereas aggression is a behavior.
   2. To help the group understand that anger is not a "bad" emotion, give them a list of ways that anger is useful and have them brainstorm. Useful functions of anger include these: (1) It energizes us. (2) It allows us to express strong emotion. (3) It helps us to feel less vulnerable and more in control of a situation. (4) It stops someone from doing something that bothers us. (5) It allows us to learn what kind of situations bother us so that we can avoid them. (6) It helps us to make necessary changes in our lives.

The Relationship Between Anger and Stress

Focus: Explore the relationship between anger and stress.

Method: Mini-lecture; develop a chart of indicators of stress.

Capsule Description: This exercise is designed to allow parents to explore the overlapping relationship between anger and stress. The group will develop a list of indicators of stress and discuss how there are various ways that different people can show they are stressed. The overlap between indicators of anger and stress can be explored by seeing how many indicators of stress would also work for anger.

   The mini-lecture will cover these main points:

1. Stress can be defined as a response that occurs when, in any situation, a person deals with something with which he or she is unfamiliar. From this definition it seems that stress is universal and that life will be full of stress because it is full of change. Possible sources of stress for adolescents include problems at home, changing schools, dating, and academic pressures. Sources of stress for parents include marital problems, conflicts with children, job-related problems, and so forth.
2. Certain changes are positive, but they are still stressful because they call for us to learn how to adapt differently.
3. Changes tend to come in clusters. One change tends to lead to other changes. This means that stress often has a tendency to "pile up." When too many changes occur too fast and stress does pile up over a short time, we are more likely to get ill or to show outward signs of stress, or both.
4. Stress is not all bad. We all need it—it adds zest to our lives and energizes us to reach goals. Think how boring life would be without change. Too much stress is disturbing, but healthful levels of stress will be different for each person.
5. Stress is caused by inner and outer circumstances. Not only do experiences outside of us cause stress, but our inner perceptions—or how we view a situation—will make us feel stress. For example, if you see someone whispering to someone else in front of you, you may feel uncomfortable, thinking that they are whispering about you—when in fact they are talking about something unrelated to you.

Have the group brainstorm a list of indicators of stress from A to Z (see Table 4.1 for examples). Ask them to come up with phrases or words describing how different people may react to stressful situations.

Once the chart is completed, lead a discussion covering how diverse these indicators can be and how many of the ways in which people show anger are also ways in which they show that they are under stress. End by suggesting that one way of dealing with anger is first to deal with your personal stress.

Identifying Sources of Stress

Focus: Identify sources of stress as well as indicators of both anger and stress.

Method: Small group exercise.

Capsule Description: The group will break up into small groups and complete Handout 1 (p. 122) ("Stress and Anger: Sources and Indicators"). This handout consists of short stories. The group needs to identify possible sources of stress and indicators of stress. These sources and indicators, which also seem to cause anger, should be listed on the handout.

WEEK 2: TRIGGERS AND CUES OF ANGER

What Are Cues and Triggers?

Focus: Define and identify cues and triggers.

Method: Mini-discussion; brainstorm a master list.

Capsule Description: This exercise is designed to help participants identify cues and triggers in their behavior. Participants will brainstorm a master list of cues and triggers.

1. A mini-lecture will be presented, which will cover the following points:

- Although anger is an emotion, there are physical signs of anger that actually occur before the emotional response. These physical signs are called *cues* because they cue us to the fact that we are getting angry.
- We can use these physical reactions as cues to start some coping techniques, like deep breathing. In this way we begin to learn to control our anger.
- Triggers can be thought of as events that make us angry. These can be direct or indirect. Direct triggers are usually things that people do to you, either in how they act or in what they say. Indirect triggers are things that we do to ourselves—in how we view a situation—that make us angry. Indirect triggers are often faulty perceptions of events.

2. Have the group brainstorm a master list of cues, direct triggers, and indirect triggers. Tell the group that there is a great deal of individual variation in how people experience anger. You can begin the brainstorming by asking the group to think of physical signs in themselves and in other people that are cues that they are getting angry.

- *Physical cues of anger:* Flushed face, sweaty palms, racing heart, glaring, clenching fist, grinding teeth, twitching, muscle tensing.
- *Direct triggers:* Jim borrows the family car without asking; a coworker blames you for something that he or she did; someone shoves you when you are waiting in line; someone honks a car horn at you and yells out the window as you drive by.
- *Indirect triggers:* Mistakenly thinking that your boss is harder

on you than on anyone else; making a "mountain out of a molehill"; focusing on bad things a friend has done and not remembering the good things.

The ABCs of Anger

Focus: Introduce the concept of analysis of events using cues, triggers, and consequences.

Method: Mini-lecture; exercise.

Capsule Description: This exercise is designed to give participants a chance to practice the ABCs of analyzing anger and to begin to think in terms of consequences.

1. A mini-lecture covering the ABC method of situational analysis will be given. The following point will be covered:

- ABC stands for *antecedents, behavior, consequences.*
- Antecedents are things that happen before we get angry. These things are like triggers.
- Behavior consists of actual reactions when we get angry.
- Consequences happen as a result of getting angry and going out of control. These may include getting into trouble with your boss, having your friends begin to avoid you, or getting hurt.

2. Ask the participants to break up into small groups. Introduce the "Anger Police" worksheet (Handout 2) for role-playing (p. 124). Each group will enact a brief scene in which someone gets angry. The rest of the group will act like police who are investigating the scene. They are interested only in the facts—the actual ABCs of the situation. Ask each group to enact situations such as these:

- Your spouse backs out of something that was promised a week ago, like taking the kids to a movie or shopping.
- Your boss asks you to work overtime when you had specifically asked to get off an hour early to go to your child's ball game.
- Your son forgot to come home directly from school to baby-sit for his younger sister.

WEEK 3: COMMUNICATION SKILLS

How People Communicate Without Talking

Focus: Explore how people use nonverbal communication in talking and listening.

Method: Mini-lecture; exercise.

Capsule Description: This session is designed to help participants become aware of nonverbal communication. The session will begin with a mini-lecture, followed by an exercise in which skills of empathic listening are identified along with a list of listening techniques.

1. The mini-lecture will cover the importance of nonverbal communication in dealing with other people. Ask one participant to portray an inconsistency between verbal and nonverbal communication and ask the group which message they attend to. For instance, a participant could act angry while saying that he or she is not angry or could act sad while saying that he or she is not sad. The concept of nonverbal behavior on the part of the listener is introduced.

2. Ask the participants to break up into groups of three. Each group will spend time with two members engaging in listening and speaking while the third member notes what behaviors showed that the listener was really listening to the speaker. Before the trios switch roles, the speakers also make notes of what the listeners did that made them feel understood. Each segment will last about 5 minutes. At the end of the exercise, reconvene the group and ask them what they noted. Body language that indicates active listening may include eye contact, some physical touching if appropriate, and leaning forward slightly toward the speaker. Other characteristics of active listening include putting aside one's own feelings for a moment and allowing the speaker to explore his or her situation without being judged. End by suggesting that active listening can be summarized as a three-step process: *stop, look,* and *listen.*

- *Step 1: Stop.* Stop talking or competing for attention and put aside your own thoughts and feelings for the moment. Take a deep breath if you need to, to help you quiet down. Choose to focus on the speaker.
- *Step 2: Look.* Look at the speaker and pay attention. Show interest by your verbal and your nonverbal communication. Observe the speaker's feelings and nonverbal communication to help you to understand the message.

- *Step 3: Listen*. Really listen to the speaker—to words and body language. Listen to the feelings as well as the content. When answering, let the speaker know, without judging or criticizing, what you heard.

Listening Exercise

1. 5 minutes:
   A observes.
   B and C talk together.
   B talks to C about one thing that was stressful today and how B coped with it.
2. 5 minutes:
   B observes.
   C and A talk.
   C starts the talk.
   C talks to A about a recent situation in which C found it hard to listen to someone else.
3. 5 minutes:
   C observes.
   A and B talk.
   A starts the talk.
   A talks to B about a situation where someone did listen whole-heartedly to A. (Adapted from Tubesing & Tubesing, 1984.)

Individual Rights and Empathic Listening

1. Discuss the difference in hearing and listening. *Listening* means hearing the meaning as well as the words.
2. Discuss the definition of *active listening*. This takes place when a person listens for the meaning of a message, then tries to express it in his or her own words.
3. Discuss the importance of listening without judging or advising.
4. Have parents role-play and have the listener repeat the message. Discuss whether body posture was congruent with the message.
5. Discuss the importance of allowing adolescents to express feelings, and parents' role in listening to the expression of feelings. Anger is a natural emotion that needs to be expressed. Relationships grow through honest expression of feelings.
6. Discuss the importance of using "I" messages instead of "you" messages in expressing feelings. Use the "I" Message Book (Handout 3, pp. 125–127) and have parents enact listening to and expressing feelings.

WEEK 4: ASSERTIVENESS TRAINING

Assertiveness

Focus: Define assertiveness and practice methods of assertiveness.

Method: Lecture; role-playing.

Capsule Description:

1. Discuss the importance of assertiveness training for parents and adolescents. How one interacts with others can be a source of stress in one's life. Assertiveness training can reduce that stress by teaching one to stand up for his legitimate rights without bullying or being bullied.

2. Discuss the three basic styles of interpersonal behavior:

- *Aggressive style:* Typical examples of aggressive behavior are fighting, accusing, threatening, and generally stepping on people without regard for their feelings. The advantage of this kind of behavior is that people do not push the aggressive person around. The disadvantage is that people do not want to be around him or her.
- *Passive style:* People are behaving passively when they let others push them around, when they do not stand up for themselves, and when they do what they are told regardless of how they feel about it. The advantage of being passive is that you rarely experience direct rejection. The disadvantage is that you are taken advantage of, and you store up a heavy burden of resentment and anger.
- *Assertive style:* People are behaving assertively when they stand up for themselves, express their true feelings, and do not let others take advantage of them. At the same time, they are considerate of others' feelings. The advantage of being assertive is that you get what you want, usually without making others mad. If you are assertive, you can act in your own best interest and not feel guilty or wrong about it. Meekness and withdrawal, attack and blame are no longer needed when you master assertive behavior. They are seen for what they are—sadly inadequate strategies of escape that create more pain and stress then they prevent. Before you can achieve assertive behavior, you must really face the fact that the passive and aggressive styles have often failed to get you what you want.

3. Discuss three basic techniques of assertiveness:

- "Broken Record": This response involves a calm repetition of what you want. There is no change in voice tone or tempo. Just keep asking calmly for what you want.
- "How to say NO": Saying "no" when you need to can prevent a buildup of anger and resentment that may later result in an outburst. When you say "no," be firm and clear. The answer should be short and to the point. Don't be overly apologetic, but if you need to, provide the person with another course of action. ("NO, I can't help you clean up your garage today. I have other things that I need to do. Maybe you can get the kids to help.")
- "Empathic Assertion": This involves sensitivity in listening to the speaker's feelings. It can be very useful when dealing with authority figures.

4. Read scenes 1–5 to participants (see Box 5.1) and have them identify A's behavior as aggressive, passive, or assertive.

5. Give out the list of mistaken traditional assumptions and legitimate rights (Handout 4, pp. 128–129). Discuss these and allow for feedback and questions.

6. Read the scenarios in Box 5.2 aloud to the group. Head some group discussion of answers to questions following each scenario.

LADDER: Steps toward Assertive Behavior

Discuss the steps toward assertive behavior using a mnemonic device: LADDER, meaning *look at, arrange, define, describe, express, reinforce.* You may find this useful in recalling these steps toward assertive behavior. The LADDER scripts below can be used to write your own problem scenes so that you can assert what you want. Initially, LADDER scripts should be written out and practiced well in advance of the situation for which they are created. Writing a script forces you to clarify your needs and increases your confidence in success.

As an example of a LADDER script, let's say that Jean wants to assert her right to half an hour each day of uninterrupted peace and quiet while she does her relaxation exercises. Her daughter Jill often interrupts with questions and attention-getting maneuvers. Jean's script goes like this.

BOX 5.1

IDENTIFYING STYLES OF INTERPERSONAL BEHAVIOR

Scene 1

A. Is that a new dent I see in the car?

B: Look, I just got home. It was a wretched day, and I don't want to talk about it now.

A: This is important to me, and we're going to talk about it now!

B: Have a heart.

A: Let's decide now who is going to pay to have it fixed, when, and where.

B: I'll take care of it. Now leave me alone, for heaven's sake!

Comment: A is aggressive. A's initial hostile statement produces resentment and withdrawal.

Scene 2

A: You left me so long by myself at that party. . . . I really felt abandoned.

B: You were being a party-pooper.

A: I didn't know anybody—the least you could have done is introduce me to some of your friends.

B: Listen, you're grown up. You can take care of yourself. I'm tired of your nagging.

A: And I'm tired of your inconsiderateness.

B: OK, I'll stick to you like glue next time.

Comment: A is aggressive. The tone is accusing and blaming. B is immediately placed on the defensive and no one wins.

Scene 3

A: Would you mind helping me for a minute with this file?

B: I'm busy with this report. Catch me later.

A: Well, I really hate to bother you, but it's important.

B: Look, I have a four o'clock deadline.

A: OK, I understand. I know it's hard to be interrupted.

Comment: A is passive. A's timid opening line is followed by complete collapse. A must now deal with the file problem alone.

BOX 5.1 *(Continued)*

IDENTIFYING STYLES OF INTERPERSONAL
BEHAVIOR *(Continued)*

Scene 4

A: I got a letter from Mom this morning. She wants to come and spend two weeks with us. I'd really like to see her.

B: Oh, no, not your mother! And right on the heels of your sister. When do we get a little time to ourselves?

A: Well, I do want her to come, but I know you need to spend some time without in-laws underfoot. I'd like to invite her to come in a month, instead of two weeks, and I think one week would be enough. What do you say to that?

B: That's a big relief to me.

Comment: A is assertive. The request is specific, non-hostile, open to negotiation, and successful.

Scene 5

A: Boy, you're looking great today!

B: Who do you think you're kidding? My hair is a fright and my clothes aren't fit for the Goodwill box.

A: Have it your way.

B: And I feel just as bad as I look today.

A: Right. I've got to run now.

Comment: A is passive. A allows the compliment to be rebuffed and surrenders to B's rush of negativity.

Script 1

- *Look at:* It's my responsibility to make sure Jill respects my needs, and I am certainly entitled to some time to myself.
- *Arrange:* I'll ask her if she is willing to discuss this problem when she gets home from school. If she isn't, we'll set a time and place to talk about it in the next day or so.
- *Define:* At least once, and sometimes more often, I'm interrupted during my relaxation exercises—even though I've shut the door and asked for the time to myself. My concentration is broken, and it becomes harder to achieve relaxation.
- *Describe:* I feel angry when my time alone is broken into, and frustrated when the exercises are then made more difficult.

BOX 5.2

SCENARIOS: ASSERTIVENESS TECHNIQUES

1. A friend borrowed $10 three weeks ago and hasn't paid you back yet.

   Your primary right is_____.
   Your friend's primary right is _____.
   A good assertiveness technique to use here is ____.

2. A friend borrowed a tape and returned it to you damaged.

   Your primary right is_____.
   Your friend's primary right is _____.
   A good assertiveness technique to use here is ____.

3. You go to the store to return a sale item you bought, which is defective.

   Your primary right is_____.
   The store's primary right is_____.
   A good assertiveness technique to use here is ____.

4. Your friend is trying to set up a blind date between your son and the child of her out-of-town friend.

   Your primary right is_____.
   Your friend's primary right is _____.
   A good assertiveness technique to use here is ____.

5. You go to a restaurant and order fish, but it comes out overdone and tasteless.

   Your primary right is_____.
   Your friend's primary right is _____.
   A good assertiveness technique to use here is ____.

Source: Adapted from Davis, Eshelmann, & McKay, 1982.

- *Express:* I would like not to be interrupted, except in a dire emergency, when my door is closed. As long as it is closed, assume that I am still doing the exercises and want to be alone.
- *Reinforce:* If I'm not interrupted, I'll come in afterward and chat with you. If I am interrupted, it will increase the time I take doing the exercises.

Here is another example. Harold has felt very reluctant to approach his boss to find out why he was turned down for a promotion. He's received no feedback about the reasons for the decision, and Harold is now feeling somewhat negative toward the company, and toward his boss in particular. Harold's script is as follows.

Script 2

- *Look at:* Resentment won't solve this. I need to assert my right to reasonable feedback from my employer.
- *Arrange:* I'll send him a memo tomorrow morning asking for time to discuss this problem.
- *Define:* I haven't gotten any feedback about the promotion. The position I applied for has been filled by someone else, and that's all I know.
- *Describe:* I felt uncomfortable not knowing at all why I didn't get it and how the decision was made.
- *Express:* So I would like to get some feedback from you about how my performance is seen, and what went into the decision.
- *Reinforce:* I think your feedback will help me do a better job.

These scripts are specific and detailed. The statement of the problem is clear and to the point, without blaming, accusing, or being passive. The feelings are expressed with "I" messages and are linked to specific events or behaviors, not to evaluations of Jean's daughter or Harold's boss. "I" messages provide a tremendous amount of safety for the assertive individual because they usually keep the other person from getting defensive or angry. You are not accusing anyone of being a bad person; you are merely stating what you want or feel entitled to. To write a successful LADDER script, do the following:

1. When appropriate, establish a mutually agreeable time and place to assert your needs.
2. Describe behavior objectively, without judging or devaluing.
3. Describe clearly, using specific references to time, place, and frequency.
4. Express your feelings calmly and directly.
5. Confine your feeling—your response—to a specific problematic behavior. Don't direct it toward the whole person.
6. Avoid delivering put-downs disguised as "honest feelings."
7. Ask for changes that are responsible, possible, and small enough not to incur a lot of resistance.
8. Ask for no more than one or two very specific changes at a time.
9. Make the reinforcements explicit, offering something that is really desirable to the other person.

10. Avoid punishments that are too big to be more than idle threats.
11. Keep your mind on your rights and goals when being assertive.

WEEK 5: SELF-INSTRUCTION TRAINING

Self-Statements and Stages of Confrontation

Focus: Define *self-statements* and identify various self-statements useful for the different stages of a confrontation.

Method: Demonstration; mini-lecture.

Capsule Description: The opening exercise, the "nine dots," is designed to show how learning to think differently can lead to new solutions. The mini-lecture will define self-statements and suggest certain helpful ones for different stages of confrontation.

1. Begin the session with the "nine dots" exercise (Figure 4.1). Draw the nine dots on the board and ask the parents to draw a figure just like that on a sheet of paper. Tell them that their task is to connect all nine dots by drawing four straight continuous lines (without lifting the pencil or retracing any lines). If any parents have solved the problem, ask them to show their solution on the board; if not, demonstrate the solution.

Ask the parents how this square affected their ability to solve the problem. It is hard to break out of the mental habit of trying to go around the square with four lines and leave the middle dot untouched. To solve the puzzle, how must they think? They need to break out of their mental habits and mental images. What effect might this same idea have on their ability to manage difficult situations?

2. The mini-lecture will introduce the concept of *self-statements* as things we say to ourselves to remind us to act in a certain way or to believe something. Show how the mind can change the emotions by describing the situation: A father has just criticized his son, and the son begins to think how unfair it was. How would the son feel? (Angry.) If, moments later, the son begins to think that maybe his father is really disappointed in him and that maybe his father doesn't love him as he used to, how would the son feel then? (Sad.) Briefly discuss the concept of taking a *perspective* as a tool parents can use to remind themselves to step back and look at and think about a problem differently.

Introduce the idea of *stages of confrontation* by writing these four stages on the board:

1. Preparing for conflict
2. Confrontation
3. Coping with arousal
4. Reflection and evaluation

Under each stage, write an adaptive thought and a maladaptive thought and ask parents how these thoughts would change a person's behavior. Examples:

- *Stage 1.* "I know I can handle this" versus "This kid is going to make me look like a fool."
- *Stage 2.* "I'll stay calm" versus "I'm going to blow this kid away."
- *Stage 3.* "I'll just relax and breathe deeply" versus "I feel really angry, and I'm going to let this kid have it."
- *Stage 4.* "I did that pretty well" versus "I can't believe I went out of control again." Or "I know these new things take time to learn, so I'll try again" versus "This stuff doesn't work. . . . just forget it!"

Self-Statements and Belief Systems

Focus: Define and explore personal belief systems and their effect on behaviors.

Method: Mini-lecture; small group exercise.

Capsule Description: A mini-lecture will introduce the concept of *belief systems*. Following this, the class will break up into small groups to work on the handout.

    1. Present the concept of belief systems as a series of self-statements upon which we act without thinking. Certain belief systems may be called the "super" syndrome, the "workaholic" syndrome, the "striving" syndrome, and the "tough" syndrome (Tubesing & Tubesing, 1984). Examples of self-statements that reflect these syndromes are: "I must always be the best." "I must work harder than anyone else." "I can always do better." "I don't care what others think of me." Ask the class to come up with other examples.

2. After breaking the class into small groups, pass out Handout 5 (p. 130). Explain that each group is to come up with a situation in which each syndrome may get one into trouble or make one feel angry. When the groups have completed this exercise, they are to write down different, more helpful self-statements for each situation.

HANDOUT 5

Positive Reinforcement

Focus: Discuss and explore the concept of positive reinforcement.

Method: Mini-lecture; homework assignment.

Capsule Description: Discussion on how behavior is controlled by reinforcement. Control of behavior. Parent effectiveness training (PET).

Behavior is controlled by rewards and punishments. If you want to
increase, strengthen, or encourage an activity or a behavior, follow it
with a reward. If you want to decrease, weaken, or discourage an activity or
behavior, punish it. The important point is that the reward or punishment
must be contingent (it comes only after the behavior has occurred).

People may control their own behaviors by giving themselves
rewards and punishments. When people do something they are proud
of—when they feel they have done well—they may treat themselves to a
reward or "pat themselves on the back." When people do something
they are not proud of—when they feel they have not done well—they
may punish themselves. Rewards and punishments can be tangible or
verbal. Self-rewards and self-punishments can be observable or private.

Pass out "Self-Rewards" (Handout 6, p. 131) and discuss it. With
the parents, stress the importance of using positive reinforcement
rather then coercion (Coats & Reynolds, 1982).

Parent Effectiveness Training (PET)

PET (Gordon, 1970) employs a "no-lose" method of resolving conflicts. In other words, it is a "no-power" method; conflicts are resolved
with no one losing. Instead, both sides win because the solution must be
acceptable to both. Parents and adolescents encounter a situation in
which their needs conflict. The parent asks the adolescent to participate with him or her in a joint search for some solution acceptable to
both. One or both may offer possible solutions. They critically evaluate
the solutions and eventually decide on a solution acceptable to both.
No "selling" is required after the solution has been selected, because
both have already accepted it. No power is required to force compli-
ance, because neither is resisting the decision.

Pass out Handout 7 (pp. 132–133), "Examples of Conflict Resolution," which illustrates the PET method. Ask for role-playing, letting one

parent make up a problem and another parent use the method to solve the problem. Discuss this afterward.

Explain that the PET method is useful for conflicts between two or more individuals. Explain that in the next session, problem solving will be explored. This will give the parents and adolescents a workable method of solving problems and helping adolescents make decisions on their own.

Review of Guidelines for Self-Reinforcement

1. Reward positive behaviors rather then criticizing yourself for failures.
2. Reward each positive behavior that meets or surpasses a contingently intermediate and as soon as possible.
3. Be generous with rewards at first.

Homework Assignment

1. Continue monitoring behaviors and recording points earned for these intermediate behaviors.
2. Be sure to trade in your points for rewards as soon as you've accumulated the contracted amount. Follow your reward menus closely. Remember: No "hoarding" of points, and no credit either!

WEEK 6: PROBLEM SOLVING

Defining Positive and Negative Methods of Coping

Focus: Define and explore both positive and negative coping mechanisms, with an emphasis on the consequences of each.

Method: Mini-lecture.

Capsule Description: The mini-lecture will cover the differences between positive and negative coping methods.

    1. Begin the session by defining a *coping mechanism* as a method we use to deal with stress and anger. We all have different coping mechanisms, and every one of us has coping methods that work—if they didn't work, we wouldn't keep using them. The problem with some coping methods is that while they may help us reduce our stress and anger initially, their long-term consequences may be negative. For instance, angry people express and reduce their anger. This may initially communicate anger and stop other people from doing whatever they were doing to make you angry, but the long-term effects may be serious. For example, people may learn to avoid a violent person; using violence often prompts violence in return, and the violent person may be hurt; and the use of violence often prompts authority figures or the police to step in. Obviously, this negative coping method may be very effective in the short run for dealing with anger-provoking situations, but in the long run its cost is very high. Positive coping methods will let you relieve stress without hurting yourself or someone else.

    2. Pass out and discuss Handout 8 "Positive and Negative Methods of Coping (p. 134)."

Methods of Dealing with Anger-Provoking Situations

Focus: Explore alternative methods for dealing with anger.

Method: Mini-lecture.

Capsule Description: A mini-lecture will be presented covering three different methods of dealing with problems: alter them, avoid them, or accept them.

Begin the lecture by discussing the three methods. All three can be effective, but the problem is knowing which one may work the best in a given situation. Illustrate each method with examples. People can *alter* a problem by changing it through assertiveness and communication skills. People can *avoid* a problem by walking away, saying "no," knowing what will be a problem, and avoiding the circumstances. People can *accept* a problem by changing their perception of it with the appropriate self-statement.

Problem Solving

Focus: Learn and apply the problem-solving method.

Method: Mini-lecture; small group exercise.

Capsule Description: The mini-lecture will cover the stages in problem solving and give the class an example of the process. The small group exercise will ask parents to use the process on their own.

1. Explain that this method can help adolescents become more independent in their decision making and thus feel more "in control" of their lives. Explain the necessity for this skill in adolescents' lives. Encourage parents to guide their adolescents in the use of this skill rather than try to solve problems for them. Stress that adolescents must choose alternatives. Begin the lecture by listing the six steps in problem solving:

- *Step 1.* State the problem. The emphasis here is on stating the problem in such a manner that it can be solved. For instance, a statement such as "My parents are mean" does not help us to solve the problem, but the statement "I need to do something about the fights I have with my parents" suggests that different alternatives are possible.
- *Step 2.* Identify your own needs as well as the needs of others involved. This will help ensure that you accept the situation and help yourself in a way that does not hurt others.
- *Step 3.* Brainstorm different alternatives, coping mechanisms, assertiveness skills, or communication skills that may help. It is useful here to remember the "three A's" of problem manage-ment. A very important step in this process is to allow any alternative to be listed, even if at first it seems silly. Silly ideas may contain important points, which can end up helping you.

- *Step 4.* List the pros and cons of each alternative. Use a plus sign (+) for each pro and a minus sign (–) for each con.
- *Step 5.* Pick an alternative to try. To see which alternative is most promising, it is easy to go back and sum up the plus and minus signs.
- *Step 6.* Evaluate your attempted solution. If that solution didn't work, go back to your list and try the next most likely alternative.

2. Write a problem on the board and lead the class in an example of the problem-solving process.

3. Have the class break up into small groups and try out the process in one or more of the examples provided in Handout 9, "Problem-Solving Exercises" (p. 135).

WEEK 7: PROGRESSIVE RELAXATION AND WRAP-UP

Methods of Progressive Relaxation

Focus: Define and practice progressions of relaxation.

Methods: Mini-lecture; exercise.

Capsule Description: Progressive relaxation techniques are discussed and practiced in group exercises.

Explain that deep muscle relaxation reduces tension and is incompatible with anxiety. Therefore, the habit of responding with relaxation blocks the habit of responding with anxiety, and vice versa.

Most people do not realize which of their muscles are chronically tense. Progressive relaxation provides a way of identifying particular muscles and muscle groups and distinguishing between sensations of tensions and deep relaxation. Four muscle groups will be covered:

1. Hands, forearms, and biceps.
2. Head, face, throat, and shoulders, with concentration on forehead, cheeks, nose, eyes, jaws, lips, tongue, and neck. Considerable attention is devoted to the head because, with regard to the emotions, the most important muscles in your body are situated in and around this region.
3. Chest, stomach, and lower back.
4. Thighs, buttocks, calves, and feet.

Teach parents to breathe in through the nose and out through the mouth. Have them get into a comfortable position in a chair or on the floor, and then read the following exercises aloud for them to follow. (The instructor may substitute any of a number of alternative commercial tapes and exercises for the following.)

- Get into a comfortable position and relax. Now clench your right fist, tighter and tighter, studying the tension as you do so. Keep it clenched and notice the tension in your fist, hand, and forearm. Now relax. Feel the looseness in your right hand, and notice the contrast with the tension. Repeat this procedure with your right fist again, always noticing, as you relax, that this is the opposite of tension. Relax and feel the difference. Repeat the entire procedure with your left fist, and then with both fists at once.

- Now bend your elbows and tense your biceps. Tense them as hard as you can and observe the feeling of tautness. Relax; straighten out your arms. Let the relaxation develop and feel the difference. Repeat this procedure, and all succeeding procedures, at least once.

- Turning your attention to your head, wrinkle your forehead as tight as you can. Now relax and smooth it out. Let yourself imagine your entire forehead and scalp becoming smooth and at rest. Now frown and notice the strain spreading throughout your forehead. Let go. Allow your brow to become smooth again. Now close your eyes. Squint them tighter. Look for the tension. Relax your eyes. Let them remain closed gently and comfortably. Now check your jaw. When the jaw is relaxed, your lips will be slightly parted. Let yourself really appreciate the contrast between tension and relaxation. Now press your tongue against the roof of your mouth. Relax. Press your lips now; purse them into an "O." Relax your lips. Notice that your forehead, scalp, eyes, jaw, tongue, and lips are all relaxed.

- Press your head back as far as it can comfortably go and observe the tension in your neck. Roll it to the right and feel the changing locus of stress. Roll it to the left. Straighten your head and bring it forward. Press your chin against your chest. Feel the tension in your throat and in the back of your neck. Relax, allowing your head to return to a comfortable position. Let the relaxation deepen. Now shrug your shoulders. Keep the tension as you hunch your head down between your shoulders. Relax your shoulders. Drop them back and feel the relaxation spreading through your neck, throat, and shoulders—pure relaxation, deeper and deeper.

- Give your entire body a chance to relax. Feel the comfort and the heaviness. Now breathe in and fill your lungs completely. Hold your breath. Notice the tension. Now exhale; let your chest become loose; let the air hiss out. Continue relaxing, letting your breath come freely and gently. Repeat this several times, noticing the tension draining from your body as you exhale. Next, tighten your stomach and hold. Note the tension, then relax. Now place your hand on your stomach. Breathe deeply into your stomach, pushing your hand up. Hold, and relax. Feel the contrast of the relaxation as the air rushes out. Now arch your back, without straining. Keep the rest of your body as relaxed as possible. Focus on the tension in your lower back. Now relax, deeper and deeper.

- Tighten your buttocks and thighs. Flex your thighs by pressing down your heels as hard as you can. Relax and feel the difference. Now curl your toes downward, making your calves tense. Study the tension. Relax. Now bend your toes toward your face, creating tension in your shins. Relax again.
- Feel the heaviness throughout your lower body as the relaxation deepens. Relax your feet, ankles, calves, shins, knees, thighs, and buttocks. Now let the relaxation spread to your stomach, lower back, and chest. Let go more and more. Experience the relaxation deepening in your shoulders, arms, and hands. Deeper and deeper. Notice the feeling of looseness and relaxation in your neck, jaws, and facial muscles. (Davis, Eshelman, & McKay, 1982)

After this exercise, have the parents discuss how it felt. Now have them close their eyes and listen to a tape about progressive relaxation. After they have experienced the tape, lead a discussion on how it affected them.

Predicting a Relapse

Focus: Identify problematic future situations that parents may be unable to handle successfully.

Method: Mini-lecture.

Capsule Description: The mini-lecture will provide some background on the normality of setbacks and provide some groundwork for coping with them.

The mini-lecture will begin by noting that the occurrence of setbacks is normal. The problem is not so much the occasional failure as our response to it. People often stop trying after failing once, thinking "I'm not able to do this." "I'll just give up." But when we try to learn any new skill, we will not be successful instantly. Think of any other skill you learned, like riding a bike. No one is able to climb up onto a bike and do wheelies the first time. Another thing that may happen to you when you first begin to try out your new behaviors is that the people who are used to seeing you get angry may actually try harder to provoke you if you don't get angry right away. Think of what happens when you put your money in a vending machine that doesn't dispense your snack. You may try putting in more money, and if that doesn't work, you may try putting in more money, and if that doesn't work, you may begin to shake the machine or to kick it to get it to do what you expect it to do.

CONCLUSION

Ask for a discussion of how the sessions have helped the class as parents. Ask if the parents have any questions about the previous sessions. Allow time for clarification of any confusing issues.

Have parents make up scenes about previous conflicts with their adolescents. Have some of them role-play to show how they would handle the situation now, while other parents act as the adolescents. Have the rest provide feedback and suggestions. Let everyone have a turn at this. Ask the parents to compare how they would have handled the situation *before* and how they would handle it *now*. Ask for feedback as to whether they feel more skilled at dealing with conflict and helping their adolescents solve problems. Also, probe for feedback about the effectiveness of support from other parents in the group. Allow time at the end of the session for closure and for expression of the group experience by parents.

PRETEST AND POSTTEST

1. True or false: Our lives would be much better if we had no stress at all.
2. The way you _____ others can change the amount of stress you feel in a certain situation.

   a. think about
   b. behave toward
   c. talk with
   d. all of the above

3. True or false: There is a strong connection between the amount of stress a person is under and how much anger he or she is likely to experience.
4. True or false: The more we feel in control of a situation, the less likely we are to feel angry or stressed out over it.
5. True or false: Whenever people get really angry, they will act aggressively.
6. True or false: Anger is a bad emotion, and we should try not to feel it.
7. One function of anger is to _____.
8. Which situation will be most likely to produce stress?

   a. something good, like moving to a nicer home where you finally have your dream backyard.
   b. something bad, like your favorite neighbor leaving and a new, very disagreeable family moving in.
   c. both a and b

9. Anger releases in our bodies a hormone called _____.
10. The signal your body sends to you that you are becoming angry is called a _____.
11. Which person will most likely act the angriest?

    a. one who thinks a long time about why he or she is angry and what to do about it.
    b. one who acts without thinking about it.

12. An event that provokes anger is called a _____.
13. An example of an indirect trigger is:

    a. someone cutting in front of you when you are in line.
    b. thinking that your boss criticized you because he or she hates you when in fact it was because you broke a rule.

14. What are the three steps in the ABC model of looking at anger?

15. True or false: One of the best ways we have of maintaining control over our lives is to be able to look at our perceptions of events.

16. List two direct triggers of your anger.

17. True or false: Talking is the only way people communicate.

18. After an angry outburst, the *least* likely outcome will be:

   a. You'll feel a lot better.
   b. You'll feel guilty.
   c. People will listen more closely to you the next time.

19. Which of these behaviors would be considered aggressive?

   a. teasing
   b. arguing
   c. threatening
   d. none of the above
   e. all of the above

20. _____ is defined as expressing your own needs clearly and firmly without hurting someone else.

21. _____ is expressing your own needs at someone else's expense.

22. What behavior is *not* included in active listening?

   a. eye contact
   b. summary statements
   c. paying attention to what's going on around you
   d. listening for the speaker's feelings

23. The assertion technique that involves a calm repetition of what you want is called the _____.

24. True or false: By being assertive we can always get what we want.

25. True or false: We can change how we feel by changing how we think.

26. If Joe believes that he must always be the best at anything he tries, how may he react to losing a major contract for his company?

27. Give two examples of positive self-statements.

28. Give two examples of negative self-statements.

29. What could you say to yourself if you feel yourself starting to become angry?

30. Match these self-statements with the stages of confrontation:

1. I handled that well.
2. My heart is pounding. . . .
   I'll start my deep breathing.
3. I know how to do this;
   I'm prepared.
4. I'm in control of myself.

a. preparing for conflict
b. reflection and evaluation
c. coping with arousal
d. confrontation

31. Describe two ways in which anger can be expressed positively or neutrally rather than aggressively.
32. The first step in problem solving is to _____.
33. True or false: Once you pick out a solution to try, you should stand by it.
34. When brainstorming in a group it is important not to _____ any of the possible solutions.
35. Name the "three A's" of dealing with problems.
36. Name two negative coping mechanisms.
37. Name two positive coping mechanisms.
38. Name all six steps in the problem-solving process in order.

ANSWERS TO PRETEST-POSTTEST

1. False
2. d
3. True
4. True
5. False
6. False
7. Various answers
8. c
9. Adrenaline
10. cue
11. b
12. trigger
13. b
14. A-antecedents
    B-behavior
    C-consequences
15. True
16. Various answers
17. False
18. c
19. e
20. Assertiveness
21. Aggressiveness
22. c
23. Broken record
24. False
25. True
26. He may become angry at himself or others.
27. Various answers
28. Various answers
29. Various answers
30. 1—b; 2—c; 3—a; 4—d
31. Various answers
32. State the problem in concrete terms.
33. False
34. Evaluate or criticize
35. Alter it; avoid it; accept it
36. Various answers
37. Various answers

38. 1. State the problem.
    2. Identify needs.
    3. Brainstorm.
    4. List pros and cons.
    5. Pick an alternative.
    6. Evaluate the attempted solution.

REFERENCES

Coats, K. I., & Reynolds, W. M. (1982). *Cognitive-behavioral therapy manual.* Madison: University of Wisconsin.

Davis, M., Eshelman, E. R., & McKay, M. (1982). *The relaxation and stress reduction workbook.* Oakland, CA: New Harbinger.

Gordon, T. (1970). *Parent effectiveness training.* New York: Van Rees.

Tubesing, N. L., & Tubesing, B. A. (1984). *Structured exercises in stress management.* (Vols. 1–3). Duluth, MN: Whole Person.

Wodarski, J. S., & Wodarski, J. S. (1993). *Curriculums and practical aspects of implementation: Preventive health services for adolescents.* Lanham, MD: University Press of America.

Wodarski, J. S. (1986). *Depression and suicide prevention by the teams-games-tournaments methods* (unpublished manual). Athens: University of Georgia School of Social Work.

HANDOUT 1

Stress and Anger: Sources and Indicators

Situation 1

John was late for work, so he skipped breakfast. He felt irritable because he had to rush so much this morning. On his way to the first meeting, in which he had a presentation he was really worried about, a coworker bumped into him, and John's papers scattered everywhere. John got mad and started yelling at the coworker.

- Possible sources of stress: _____
- Stress indicators: _____
- Stress indicators which may also signal anger: _____

Situation 2

Sue's parents have been fighting with each other for a month now. Sue spends a lot of time in her room watching TV, trying to block out the noise of her parents' arguments. She is feeling pretty depressed over this. She is still doing OK in school, but her friends have noticed that she is gaining weight and that she gets a lot of headaches. They are worried about her.

- Possible sources of stress: _____
- Stress indicators: _____
- Stress indicators which may also signal anger: _____

Situation 3

Beth and her family have just moved into town. Beth is still sulking because she left all her friends behind. She was just starting to get to know some cute boys, and now her parents decide to move. She doesn't care if her father's company transferred him; she's mad about leaving everything she knows behind her. Beth has even thrown some tantrums so that her parents will understand how hard this is for her. The thought of starting over in a new school gives her knots in her stomach.

- Possible sources of stress: _____
- Stress indicators: _____
- Stress indicators which may also signal anger: _____

Situation 4

Larry has been complaining to Ann about everything lately. Ann is not sure what's going on, but she knows that Larry is working a lot more than usual. When he finally does come home, he looks worried and has no energy. When Larry is at home, he seems really restless and cranky.

- Possible sources of stress: _____
- Stress indicators: _____
- Stress indicators which may also signal anger: _____

HANDOUT 2

Worksheet: "Anger Police"

| Role-Playing # | Antecedents | | Behavior | | Consequences |
	Direct Triggers	Possible Indirect Triggers	Cues	Action Taken	

HANDOUT 3

The "I" Message Book

Three parts of "I" messages:

1. I feel _____
   (an emotion)

2. When you_____
   (action of others)

3. Because _____
   (how action affects you)

Words for expressing *anger*

annoyed	teed off
put out	bugged
upset with	pissed off
irritated	resentful
burned	furious

Words for expressing *hurt*

taken for granted	let down
unappreciated	put down
neglected	used
mistreated	betrayed
criticized	crushed
wounded	

Words for expressing *confusion*

uneasy	uncomfortable
bothered	unsure
uncertain	disturbed
frustrated	lost
troubled	mixed-up
puzzled	ambivalent

Words for expressing *anxiety*

insecure	self-conscious
worried	uncomfortable
shy	awkward
shaky	nervous
tense	uptight
defensive	scared
afraid	desperate

Words for expressing *inadequacy*

uncertain	unimportant
small	incapable
clumsy	stupid
inferior	like a failure
helpless	worthless

Words for expressing *depression*

sad	down
low	unhappy
lousy	gloomy
hopeless	awful
rotten	miserable

Words for expressing *guilt*

blew it	goofed
at fault	wrong
silly	ridiculous
foolish	ashamed
horrible	humiliated
unforgivable	sick at heart

Words for expressing *loneliness*

excluded	left out
shut out	alone
rejected	alienated
cut off	isolated

Words for expressing *strength*

can cope	up to it
important	in control
successful	capable
able	effective
committed	inspired
determined	confident

Words for expressing *happiness*

calm	fulfilled
satisfied	good
wonderful	super
enthusiastic	excited
terrific	fantastic

Words for expressing *love*

accept	like
friendly	value
trust	concern for
admire	respect
fond of	affection for
devoted to	cherish

HANDOUT 4

Mistaken Traditional Assumptions and Legitimate Rights

Mistaken Assumptions	*Your Legitimate Rights*
1. It is selfish to put your needs before others' needs.	You have a right to put yourself first sometimes.
2. It is shameful to make mistakes. You should have an appropriate response for every occasion.	You have a right to make mistakes.
3. If you can't convince others that your feelings are reasonable, then they must be wrong, or maybe you are going crazy.	You have a right to be the final judge of your feelings and accept time as legitimate.
4. You should respect the views of others, especially if they are in a position of authority. Keep your differences of opinion to yourself. Listen and learn.	You have a right to have your own opinions and convictions.
5. You should always try to be logical and consistent.	You have a right to change your mind or decide on a different course of action.
6. You should be flexible and adjust. Others have good reasons for their actions and it's not polite to question them.	You have a right to protest unfair treatment or criticism.
7. You should never interrupt people. Asking questions reveals your stupidity.	You have a right to interrupt in order to ask for clarification.
8. Things could get worse. Don't rock the boat.	You have a right to negotiate for change.
9. You shouldn't take up others' valuable time with your problems.	You have a right to ask for help or emotional support.

10. People don't want to hear that you feel bad, so keep it to yourself.

You have a right to feel and express pain.

11. When people take the time to give advice, you should take it very seriously. They are often right.

You have a right to ignore the advice of others.

12. Knowing that you did something well is its own reward. People don't like show-offs. Successful people are secretly disliked and envied. Be modest when when complimented.

You have a right to receive formal recognition for your work and your achievements.

13. You should always try to accommodate others. If you don't, they won't be there when you need them.

You have a right to say "no."

14. Don't be antisocial. People are going to think you don't like them if you say you'd rather be alone instead of with them.

You have the right to be alone, even if others would prefer your company.

15. You should always have a good reason for what you feel and do.

You have a right not to have to justify yourself to others.

16. When people are in trouble, you should help them.

You have a right not to take responsibility for someone else's problem.

17. You should be sensitive to the needs and wishes of others, even when they are unable to tell you what they want.

You have a right not to have to anticipate others' needs and wishes.

18. It's always a good policy to stay on people's good side.

You have a right not to always worry about the goodwill of others.

19. It's not nice to put people off. If questioned, give an answer.

You have a right to choose not to respond to a situation.

HANDOUT 5

Exercise: Belief Systems

1. *"Super" Syndrome*
   I always have to be the best.
   I can always do better than everyone else.

   - A situation where these beliefs could make you mad: _____
   - A more helpful set of self-statements would be: _____

2. *"Workaholic" Syndrome*
   I must work harder than everyone else all the time.
   I'm only worth as much as I accomplish.

   - A situation where these beliefs could make you mad: _____
   - A more helpful set of self-statements would be: _____

3. *"Striving" Syndrome*
   I must always try harder.
   No matter what I've done, I could have done better.

   - A situation where these beliefs could make you mad: _____
   - A more helpful set of self-statements would be: _____

4. *"Tough" Syndrome*
   I don't show it when I'm hurt.
   I don't need anyone else.

   - A situation where these beliefs could make you mad: _____
   - A more helpful set of self-statements would be: _____

HANDOUT 6

Exercise: Self-Rewards

Outline the self-reinforcement procedure for parents and then review each step in detail to be sure they understand the assignment.

Instructions

1. On the "Rewards Menu" form, list as many potential rewards for yourself as you can. Rewards should:

   a. be truly enjoyable
   b. vary in magnitude from large to small
   c. be freely administered; i.e., you should be able to decide when and where they occur.

   Note that activities as well as things can be rewards. One principle you can use is that easy positive activities can be used to reward hard positive activities. Examples of positive rewards that you can give to yourself include:

   - Material rewards (clothes, books, etc.)
   - Activities (going to a movie, to a park, or shopping; going to an enjoyable class; swimming; watching a favorite show; eating a favorite food).

2. Now assign "prices" to the items on your reward menu. Give each item a value (1 to 10) indicating how "big" a reward it would be for you.
3. Now assign point values to your intermediate goals on your goal-setting worksheets. Give each item a value (1 to 10). This indicates how many points you should earn for each activity. Be generous! You can always reduce the points later if an activity turns out to be easier than you thought.
4. As you earn points by reaching your intermediate goals, reward this progress by spending your points on your reward menu. Keep a total of points earned and spent on a self-monitoring log. Reward is more effective if it is immediate, so cash in your points as often as possible. Remember the principle: Reward should be contingent on performing a behavior. Your reward came because of the behavior. The points simply make it easier to translate one into the other.
5. Are there any questions?

HANDOUT 7

Examples of Conflict Resolution

Scenario 1

Jane:	Bye. I'm off to school.
Father:	Honey, it's raining outside and you don't have your raincoat on.
Jane:	I don't need it.
Father:	I think it's raining quite hard, and I'm concerned that you'll ruin your clothes or get a cold, and that will affect us.
Jane:	Well, I sure don't want to wear my raincoat.
Father:	You sure sound as though you definitely don't want to wear that raincoat.
Jane:	That's right—I hate it!
Father:	You really hate your raincoat.
Jane:	Yeah, it's plaid.
Father:	Something about plaid raincoats you hate, huh?
Jane:	Yes, nobody at school wears plaid raincoats.
Father:	You don't want to be the only one wearing something different.
Jane:	I sure don't. Everybody wears plain-colored raincoats—either white or blue or green.
Father:	I see. Well, we really have a conflict here. You don't want to wear your raincoat 'cause it's plaid, but I sure don't want to pay a cleaning bill, and I will not feel comfortable about your getting a cold. Can you think of a solution that we both could accept? How could we solve this so we're both happy?
Jane:	(Pause.) Maybe I could borrow Mom's raincoat today.
Father:	What does that look like? Is it plain-colored?
Jane:	Yeah, it's white.
Father:	Do you think she will let you wear it today?
Jane:	I'll ask her. (Comes back in a few minutes with the jacket on; sleeves are too long, but she rolls them back.) It's OK by Mom.
Father:	You're happy with that thing?
Jane:	Sure, it's fine.
Father:	Well, I'm convinced it will keep you dry. So if you're happy with that solution, I am too.
Jane:	Well, so long.
Father:	So long. Have a good day at school.

What happened here? Obviously, Jane and her father resolved their conflict to the satisfaction of both. It was resolved rather quickly, too. The father did not have to waste time being an imploring sales-man, trying to sell his solution. No power was involved—either on the part of the father or on the part of Jane. Finally, both walked away from the problem solving, feeling warmth toward each other. The father could say "Have a good day at school" and really mean it, and Jane could go to school free of the fear of embarrassment over a plaid raincoat.

Scenario 2

Mother:	Cindy, I'm sick and tired of nagging you about your room, and I'm sure you're tired of my getting on your back about it. Occasionally you clean it up, but mostly it's a mess and I'm mad. Let's try a new method I've learned in class. Let's see if we can find a solution we both will accept—one that will make us both happy. I don't want to make you clean your room and have you be unhappy with that, but I don't want to be embarrassed and uncomfortable and be mad at you either. How could we solve this problem once and for all? Will you try?
Cindy:	Well, I'll try but I know I'll just end up having to keep it clean.
Mother:	No. I am suggesting we find a solution that would definitely be acceptable to both, not just to me.
Cindy:	Well, I've got an idea. You hate to cook but like cleaning, and I hate cleaning and love to cook. And besides, I want to learn more about cooking. What if I cook two dinners a week for you and Dad and me if you clean up my room once or twice a week?
Mother:	Do you think that would work out—really?
Cindy:	Yes, I'd really love it.
Mother:	OK, then let's give it a try. Are you also offering to do the dishes?
Cindy:	Sure.
Mother:	OK. Maybe now your room will get cleaned according to my own standards. After all, I'll be doing it myself.

HANDOUT 8

Positive and Negative Methods of Coping

Negative Coping	Positive Coping
Using drugs and alcohol	Looking for humor in the situation
Pretending nothing is wrong	Exercising
Using aggressive or violent behavior	Eating healthful foods
	Using relaxation
Always imagining that the worst thing will happen	Using positive self-statements
	Using assertiveness
Going on a spending spree	Playing music or an instrument
Bingeing on food	Playing a game
Getting even, getting revenge	Relabeling and changing your perspective
Demanding your own way	
Complaining	Sharing your feelings in a way that won't hurt others
Criticizing	

HANDOUT 9

Problem-Solving Exercises

Problem 1

You are at a store shopping for some last-minute Christmas gifts for your friends and family. The store is very crowded, and people seem to be tense. You have finally found what you want, and as you walk up to the checkout, an older woman rushes past you, knocking your gifts out of your arms and cutting in front of you in line.

Problem 2

Your dad is on your back about something all the time. He doesn't like your friends, so he won't let you hang out with them. But he also says he won't pick your friends for you.

Problem 3

You and your daughter are always fighting over the bathroom you share. Not only does she hog the bathroom in the morning when you have to get to work, but she leaves it filthy. You're fed up with the situation, and now it seems as though you're angry with her all day.

Chapter 6

Violent Youth: A Critical Challenge for Parents, Schools, and the Community

Lisa A. Rapp

Violent behavior is a public health concern that affects all members of our society. Every year in the U.S., more than 20,000 people die and more than 2.2 million suffer injuries from violent behaviors. Young people are disproportionately represented among the perpetrators and among the victims of this violence. Reports have consistently shown that persons 15 to 34 years of age have the highest rates of homicide of any age group (Rosenberg, 1995).

Despite the vast amount of information we have on juvenile violence, we have made little impact on this tragic social problem. Instead, studies have indicated that the rate and severity of juvenile violence have increased in the last 30 years (Earls, 1994). Interventions that have failed in the past have failed on two levels: First, they have not offered long-term solutions to the problems of violence; second, they have intervened on only one level. In other words, these programs have not taught young people the skills they need to survive and develop into productive citizens, and these programs have intervened only with youngsters, excluding peers, parents, schools, and communities.

The evidence suggests that intervention and prevention programs need to begin early, need to intervene on many levels, and need to give youngsters specific skills to learn and utilize in their environment. The expansive efforts needed to begin such programs will be worth the almost inconceivable benefits.

The Teams-Games-Tournaments (TGT) technique has been presented here as an appropriate, effective educational approach that intervenes with young people, their families, and the community to reduce juvenile violence. This cognitive-behavioral group method focuses on helping youngsters make responsible decisions regarding aggressive behavior and substance abuse. In addition, the TGT program emphasizes education of parents about problem solving and communication. This program is realistic and easy to implement.

The TGT curriculum—which concentrates on peer influence—is particularly effective in teaching adolescents about violent behavior and substance abuse. That is because the data have repeatedly indicated that these social problems are related to peer influence and usually occur within a group context. This curriculum provides young people with feasible techniques for resisting peer pressure and improving social skills.

SCHOOLS AND PEERS

Since young people spend the majority of their time in a school setting, the school system seems to be a natural forum for imparting knowledge and implementing change (Wodarski & Wodarski, 1995). The school setting is a natural link between parents, youngsters, and the community. Educational and preventive programs can be started early to instill positive attitudes regarding conflict resolution and substance abuse. Teachers and staff who teach and exhibit these attitudes and behaviors can be positive role models for the youth they work with.

PARENTS AND FAMILIES

Juveniles need reinforcement and guidance from trusted, loving adults in addition to the support they receive from teachers and staff. Parents must be informed that they have the right and the responsibility to establish structure and discipline in the home. The TGT approach assists parents with discipline, communication, and coping skills, so that they in turn can help their children. Lack of consistency and lack of structure in parenting have been found to be among the greatest risk factors for later violent behavior and substance abuse (Vuchinich, Bank, & Patterson, 1992). In addition, excessive criticism, negative statements, threats, and corporal punishment by parents can also increase violent behavior and substance abuse. It is imperative that parents be educated about positive communication and interaction with their children.

The curriculum for parents is intended to provide them with the information and skills they need to handle juvenile violence and substance abuse. Through this curriculum, parents learn to set clear guidelines regarding anger and substance abuse. Parents also learn techniques for enforcing consequences and communicating appropriately with their children. These positive skills can help to offset the negative influences that surround our youth today.

COMMUNITY AND MEDIA

The media can send extremely powerful messages, and adolescents are more susceptible than adults to these influences. Strasburger (1989) found that young people watch approximately 20 to 25 hours of television per week. Often, harmful messages about violent behavior as well as substance abuse are portrayed through the media. MTV, soap operas, and sitcoms depict substance abuse as commonplace and violent behavior as "cool." In reality, juveniles need to be informed that substance abuse can lead to serious harm and violent behavior can lead to death.

Juveniles need positive role models to impart societal norms, and these role models need to come from the home and the community. Communities need to support parents in raising youngsters and reinforce nonviolence and avoidance of substance abuse. Community support of school-based preventive efforts is imperative if these interventions are to have an impact on young people.

In order to change and prevent violent behavior and substance abuse, interventions must be focused on all systems that influence young people. These include peers, parents, families, schools, media, and the community. Single-pronged approaches are ineffectual. The TGT provides a curriculum that can help us in this endeavor; it targets multiple systems on multiple levels. To make a critical impact on juvenile violence, this type of multisystemic intervention is necessary.

REFERENCES

Earls, F. (1994). Violence and today's youth. *Future of Children, 4,* 10–23.

Rosenberg, M. (1995). Violence in America: An integrated approach to under-standing prevention. *Journal of Health Care for the Poor and Underserved, 6,* 102–112.

Strasburger, V. (1989). Children, adolescents, and television: The role of pedia-tricians. *Pediatrics, 83,* 446.

Vuchinich, S., Bank, L., & Patterson, G. (1992). Parenting, peers, and the stability of antisocial behavior in preadolescent boys. *Developmental Psychology, 28,* 510–520.

Wodarski, L., & Wodarski, J. (1995). *Adolescent sexuality: A comprehensive peer/parent curriculum.* Springfield, IL: Thomas.

Index

SP *Springer Publishing Company*

Challenging Family Therapy Situations
Perspectives in Social Construction

Joan D. Atwood, PhD, Editor

This book provides a leading-edge therapeutic approach to family therapy situations through its use of social construction theory emphasizing the role of language and social environment. It focuses on the most current theoretical issues in family therapy, applies recent theory to difficult family situations, and presents practical techniques and information on special issues in the field.

Each chapter follows basic social construction assumptions, putting solution-focused techniques into practical, understandable language. The topics included—extramarital affairs, AIDS, depression, suicide, violence, divorce, and chronic illness—are among the most common problems that therapists encounter. Both students and seasoned family therapists will gain a new view of what knowledge and skills they might need when confronted with clients dealing with any one of the problems identified in the book.

Contents:
Social Construction Theory and Therapy, *J.D. Atwood* • Extramarital Affairs and Constructed Meanings: A Social Constructionist Therapeutic Approach, *J.D. Atwood and M. Seifer* • AIDS and the Family Narrative: Reconstructing A Story to Encompass An Illness, *N. Cohan* • Depression: Constructing the Flip Side of the Coin, *T. Pakula and J.D. Atwood* • Suicide: Constructing Hope, *J.D. Atwood* • Dueling Couples, *G.J. Meyer* • Physical Violence in the Family, *J.D. Atwood* • Intimacy Dissolution: Divorce, *J.D. Atwood* • When a Loved One Has a Chronic Illness, *E. Weinstein and J.D. Atwood*

1997   296pp   0-8261-9820-1   hardcover

536 Broadway, New York, NY 10012-3955 • (212) 431-4370 • Fax (212) 941-7842

⑤ *Springer Publishing Company*

Family Violence and Men of Color
Healing the Wounded Male Spirit
Ricardo Carrillo, PhD and **Jerry Tello,** Editors

"Family Violence and Men of Color is the best book on cross-cultural issues and domestic violence that I have ever read. It is a good combination of literature review, clinical interventions, and cultural imagery that will not only inform the reader but help them develop a true appreciation for the essence of different cultures."
    —Daniel Sonkin, PhD, Marriage, Family, and Child Counselor

"This innovative book examines an important, timely topic...and makes an original contribution to existing literature in the area of domestic violence. The content will greatly enhance practitioners and students' understanding and skills in working with men of color, especially in situations involving domestic violence."
    —Elaine P. Congress, DSW, Director of the Doctoral Program
        Associate Professor, Fordham University Graduate School of
                                                    Social Service

Providing a culturally integrated perspective of this controversial subject, this volume offers great insight found in the case studies and storytelling of men in their communities. Research reviewed includes the prevalence of homicide, child abuse, and domestic violence in special populations, including African American, Latino/Chicano, Asian American, and Native American.

Contents:
- Violence in Communities of Color
- The Noble Man Searching for Balance
- Clinical Treatment of Latino Domestic Violence Offenders
- A Post-colonial Perspective on Domestic Violence in Indian Country
- Healing and Confronting the African American Batterer
- Asian American Domestic Violence: A Critical Psychohistorical Perspective
- Asian Men and Violence
- Epilogue

1998   192pp   0-8261-1173-4   *hardcover*

536 Broadway, New York, NY 10012-3955 • (212) 431-4370 • Fax (212) 941-7842

Springer Publishing Company

Battered Women and Their Families, 2nd Edition
Intervention Strategies and Treatment Programs
Albert R. Roberts, PhD, Editor

"...a landmark achievement. This is the first comprehensive book to examine domestic violence from a multi-cultural perspective. This brilliantly written and all-inclusive resource provides new clinical knowledge and practice wisdom to alleviate the emotional pain and trauma of battered women and their children. I have been searching for a book like this for years, especially when I was Consultant to the Army Surgeon General."

—Jesse J. Harris, PhD, BCD, ACSW
Professor and Dean, School of Social Work, University of Maryland
Colonel, Retired

"This volume provides the step-by-step answers and solutions on how to detect, assess, and treat battered women in trauma, acute crisis, and/or emergency situations. Professor Roberts' timely volume provides concrete solutions and a non-judgmental approach to a major societal and public health problem. If you are planning to purchase only one book on interpersonal violence this year, this is the essential book to purchase."

—Karil S. Klingbeil, MSW, ACSW
*Director, Dept. of Social Work, Harborview Medical Center
Clinical Associate Professor, University of Washington, School of Social Work*

Partial Contents:
Crisis Intervention and Cognitive Problem-Solving Therapy with Battered Women: A National Survey and Practice Model, *A.R. Roberts and S. Burman* • The Stress-Crisis Continuum: Its Application to Domestic Violence, *P.V. Valentine, A.R. Roberts and A.W. Burgess* • Crisis Intervention with Traumatized Child Witnesses in Shelters for Battered Women, *P. Lehmann and B.E. Carlson* • Battered Women in the Emergency Room: Emerging Roles for the ER Social Worker and Clinical Nurse Specialist, *M.E. Boes* • Elder Abuse, *P. Brownell and I. Abelman* • Application of the Culturagram to Assess and Empower Culturally and Ethnically Diverse Battered Women, *P. Brownell and E.P. Congress* • Validating Coping Strategies and Empowering Latino Battered Women in Puerto Rico, *D. Valle Ferrer*

1998   552pp   0-8261-4591-4   hardcover

536 Broadway, New York, NY 10012-3955 • (212) 431-4370 • Fax (212) 941-7842

SP *Springer Publishing Company*

Crisis Intervention and Trauma Response
Theory and Practice

Barbara Rubin Wainrib, EdD
Ellin L. Bloch, PhD

Crisis
Intervention
and Trauma
Response

THEORY AND PRACTICE

Barbara Rubin Wainrib
Ellin L. Bloch

Springer Publishing Company

"The doctor said that the surgery on my wife's cancer was a failure and that there was nothing more that they could do. I felt as if I was in a bad movie, and everything around me had come to a halt."
—James G., husband of a cancer victim

Crisis Intervention and Trauma Response offers short-term, problem-oriented, therapeutic interventions formulated to produce constructive change for the client as quickly and directly as possible. Presenting their successful General Crisis Response model for intervention, the authors use actual case examples like James G. to encourage therapists to focus on clients' inner strengths and cope with the immediate crisis. The book is filled with exercises to develop techniques for building verbal and non-verbal skills, and awareness of individual and cultural differences. A Crisis and Trauma Assessment checklist is included for effective therapeutic interventions, whether in your office or at a trauma site.

Contents: • About this Book
• Crisis, Trauma, and You:
  Theories of Crisis and Trauma
• How We Respond to Crisis and Trauma
• Principles and Models of Intervention
• Assessment for Crisis and Trauma
• Suicide and Violence:
  Assessment and Intervention
• Putting it All Together: The Pragmatics

1998   176pp (est.)   0-8261-1175-0   softcover

536 Broadway, New York, NY 10012-3955 • (212) 431-4370 • Fax (212) 941-7842